Why We Won:
The American Revolution

Why We Won:
The American Revolution

John Barry Flynn

Aventine Press

Copyright © May, 2004 by John Barry Flynn
First Edition

Without limiting the rights under copyright reserved above, no part of this publication may be reproduced, stored in or introduced into a retrieval system, or transmitted, in any form or by any means (electronic, mechanical, photocopying, recording, or otherwise), without the prior written permission of both the copyright owner and the publisher of this book.

Published by Aventine Press
1202 Donax Ave Suite 12
Imperial Beach, CA 91932, USA

www.aventinepress.com

ISBN: 1-59330-168-5
Printed in the United States of America
ALL RIGHTS RESERVED

A Dedication

To the men and women whose sacrifices created this inspiring story and to Nathan and Abraham whose love of stories inspired me to write it.

TABLE of CONTENTS

Preamble - The Story..1

Chapter 1. Outcasts and Adventurers......................5

Chapter 2. Setting the Stage....................................17
    The French and Indian War............................19
    Who's Boss?...22

Chapter 3. War...27
    Lexington and Concord..................................32
    Ticonderoga...37
    Bunker Hill...38
    Boston..46
    A Serious Misjudgment.................................46

Chapter 4. Washington's Hard Lesson...................49
    Brooklyn - The Empire Strikes Back..............51

Chapter 5. Hard Times..55

Chapter 6. Burgoyne's Ambitious Plan...................59

Chapter 7. Ticonderoga Revisited...........................65
    A Walk Through the Forest............................68

Chapter 8. Trouble in the West...............................69

Chapter 9. A Promise Kept - Bennington................73

Chapter 10. The Most Important Battle - Saratoga...77
    The End Game..81

Chapter 11. World War...89

Chapter 12. The Enigma of Benedict Arnold....................93

Chapter 13. Interlude..103

Chapter 14. The War Moves South...............................107
    Charleston...111
    Camden and Gates - More Bad News..................112
    A Ray of Hope - King's Mountain.......................113
    Reintroducing Nathaniel Greene..........................115
    Daniel Morgan Again! - Cowpens........................116
    Back to Square One..119

Chapter 15. Gotcha!...121

Chapter 16. How It Finally Ended................................127
    Washington's Greatness......................................132

Appendix 1. Table of Dates...137

Appendix 2. Cast of Characters...................................139

Appendix 3. The Saratoga Surrender Sequence.............175

Bibliography..177

Endnotes...181

Index..183

Preamble

The Story

"What's happenin'?"
"Nothin' good, Grampa."

"What's wrong? What are you doing?"
"Studyin'"
"Studying for what?"
"History. American history."

"What period in American history?"
"'What period?', you talk like our teacher. The Revolution."

"The Revolution! That's one of the greatest periods - excuse the term. Why don't you like it?"
"It's bogus. Just memorizing a lot of useless dates and names. I'll probably forget them the day after the test."
"Or shortly thereafter. That's sad.
Is that all you talk about in class?"
"Oh, we talk about other things but the tests are what count."

"The important question in history is 'why?', not 'what?' or 'when?'. The 'whats' and 'whens' are only there to stitch the story together."

"But there's so much to know - all that stitching takes a lot of thread."

"Sure, if you want to include all the details; there were thousands of incidents, raids, battles, and intrigues. But I'll bet that you can understand the American Revolution in about six steps.

With that base, everything else can be added according to your needs and interests. Needs like passing tests.

To me, it's the most stirring, most exciting story ever - it's about how this great country came to be. It has all the elements of a great story: a theme that is grand in scope and impact, heroism, villainy, drama, surprise, a heartwarming outcome, and a great cast of characters."

"What drama?"

"Well ... a solid British plan to nip the Revolution at Bunker Hill foiled by a seasoned veteran and his New Hampshire frontiersmen, British caution and a fortuitous fog allowing our army to escape from Brooklyn, a dashing general who later became a traitor, an Irish sharpshooter, and a pivotal victory at Saratoga ... for example."

"It doesn't sound like the same story I've been reading - except, maybe, the characters. I think I'd better keep memorizing for now, but if I ride to the family picnic in your car, could you tell it to me as we go? We always did like to hear your stories - especially about when you were a boy."

"Like when I had to walk for miles to get to school? Through the deep snow?"

"Ha...uphill...both ways!"

"OK, it's a date; but just to get you thinking, the six pieces of the story are:
- The people and their poor relationship with the Crown.
- The events that proceeded the Revolution, especially the Seven Year's War.
- The first battles.
- Saratoga
- The war in the South.
- Yorktown.

It really is a fascinating story - world shaping events leading to who we are and how our society came to be; human nature at its best and worst; great challenge and sacrifice; and a lot of what some call 'luck'."

"But you don't call it luck?"

"No, not really. Opportunities arise continuously and capable people recognize them and exploit them.

It was certainly fortunate that people like Washington, Franklin, Adams, Jefferson, Greene and so many others were there when we needed them, but calling it luck suggests that the Revolution was independent of them. These people created the Revolution; they were its progenitor and soul; without them it wouldn't have happened when it did.

This was a new land with New World spirit and daring, stimulated by adversity and the freedom to confront challenges directly, unencumbered by Old World strictures."

"So there's no such thing as luck?"

"Oh, I won't go that far. It was lucky for us when Napoleon's army died of fever in Haiti - but that's a different story."

Chapter 1
Outcasts and Adventurers

"All set?"
"Let's go."

"First, we have to consider why the early American settlers came here and what kind of people they were."

The original European settlers in America were, mostly, outcasts from England, although they also included others - adventurers seeking trade, gold, or just a better chance in life.

The latter group were English, French, Dutch, German, Scottish, Irish, and Swedish, among others.

The most common reason for the outcasts' nettlesome reputation in England was their opposition to the Church of England. The seriousness of this opposition is not intuitively grasped by the Americans of today. We constitutionally hold all churches apart from the affairs of State, although various sects have, perhaps, too much influence over the legislation of individual states.

In England, opposition to the Church was disloyalty to the State.

Our story begins in 17th century England where the Church and State were so totally bound together that all citizens were obliged to support the Church, as an extension of the Realm, regardless of their own religious affiliations. The Church instigated legislation and could, therefore, be used as an agent of those who sought political favors. The Church felt that it should be above criticism from other sects and used its political power to suppress them. The secular authorities acted against the "troublemakers" sowing dissension among many of the English people.

So an accommodation was made that, for the time, seemed to solve a number of problems simultaneously - encourage resettlement of the dissenters to North America.

Think of it! In one stroke of policy, implemented over many years, the British Crown could:
- Distance itself from its critics, relieve the pressure that it must have felt from the established Church hierarchy to do something about these holier-than-thou troublemakers, and promote harmony in the Realm.

- Establish a buffer against competing European settlements to the north and south in North America.

Interestingly, these competing French and Spanish settlements were primarily commercial, backed by a military presence. They mostly wanted the furs and fish from the north and the gold and profitable spices (also attractive to the British and French) from the south and were disinclined to compete with the fierce and numerous native inhabitants for the forests and farmlands of the mid-continent.

These same natives had successfully discouraged Viking settlement long before.

- Discharge debts owed by the Crown to some of the leaders of minority sects. What a deal! - selling profitless land with no real title for real money.

"I thought that the natives helped the settlers."

"You remember well. At first the natives (the Europeans misnamed them Indians) in the Plymouth Colony helped the settlers and had a treaty of peace that the leaders on both sides tried hard to respect. But when the native leader, Massasoit, died the peace didn't hold.

Georgia and Pennsylvania also experienced good relations with the natives, again due to exceptional leadership.

In some other colonies, especially Virginia, there was fighting from the beginning."

"Why did Massasoit want to help?"

"Because he thought it would help his people. They were under attack from other tribes and had been weakened considerably by sickness from European diseases. The guns of the settlers were the counterbalancing strength that he needed.

Also, trade provided goods that somewhat enhanced the living standard of the tribe. But he didn't realize how many other settlers would come flooding in behind them."

"Wasn't there enough room for everybody?"

"There might have been if everyone lived in the European manner which supported a greater population density than the native style. The Europeans could rely upon domesticated crops and animals for their food while the natives were much more dependent upon hunting and the gathering of 'wild' foods.

If the English had lived entirely on their small farms their relationship with the natives would have been better. But they began to also gather from nature's limited bounty and what they took impacted the natives directly. Every deer that was shot and every forest tree that was turned into firewood made the natives poorer.

Some natives adopted the ways and religion of the newcomers and struggled for survival and acceptance in English society. Undoubtedly, many of their genes are in today's American pool. The others were eventually forced westward or northward, usually after spirited but futile resistance.

The phenomenon of displacement of native peoples had occurred countless times in the settlement of the world and on every habitable continent. Usually, the tribes with more military capability overcame and destroyed, displaced, or absorbed the weaker tribes.

Respect for international boundaries and the property rights of others is a very new concept. "Justice" is an ideal readily abandoned or rationalized away when opposed by stronger motivations, like greed. Although 'wrong' by today's slowly emerging standards, the displacement and destruction of the North American natives was natural by the standards of the those times and, sadly, is still not uncommon in parts of today's world.

Many of the disputes between natives and settlers were due to the indifference, intransigence, and sometimes criminal actions of the settlers. Many simply saw nothing other than their own needs, laws, customs, and loyalties.

Others, particularly the Pennsylvania Quakers, had a much better relationship with the natives."

"The settlers were to blame for the trouble?"

"Simplistically, and viewed by today's standards, yes.

At best, they applied their own laws to acquire land from people who knew too little about the process and who had a questionable right to sell. These sales were then enforced by superior arms, tactics, and technology.

At worst, the natives were cheated, coerced, intoxicated, sickened and destroyed in the settlers' pursuit of land. The legal system rarely sought justice for the natives.

Undoubtedly, many Englishmen who considered themselves to be scrupulously moral rationalized their behavior by viewing the natives as inferior beings and the settlement of their lands as English destiny.

It was a manifestation of God's will and pleasure.

More than two centuries later the westward bound Mormons, using their own trail and their own moral code, avoided the conflict that others had with the natives. Conflict is avoidable.

Despite what we would prefer to believe, some very unprincipled and violent people were among those who settled this land."

In the midst of the English settlers, the Dutch (and Germans) quietly and effectively created a successful colony based on both agriculture and commerce along the Hudson River in what is now New York State. The British eventually absorbed this enclave[1] within their colonies without displacing or penalizing the settlers, although the change in government was not welcome and the Dutch mostly supported the Revolution when it came.

The British reimbursed the Dutch government for its loss with a small island rich in nutmeg, a spice thought to protect against plague and thereby eagerly sought by Europeans rightly terrified by the disease. The spice may have actually helped by repelling the fleas that carried the plague bacteria.[2]

The reimbursement may have been the only option for the Dutch since they couldn't hope to defend their small enclave militarily against a continent of British. It was an offer that they couldn't refuse.

It is ironic that the same separatists and dissenters that aggravated England should become the raw material for the new British settlements.

Once established, the British colonies became a destination for other minorities, chiefly Continental European Protestants, but also some Catholics and Jews.

It has been speculated that these self-selected risk-taking settlers created an emotionally, perhaps genetically, distinct people that were particularly suited to the task of embracing freedom and absorbing a continent.

The only "immigrants" who did not fit this pattern were the African slaves who were taken against their wishes. The horrors of slavery aside, those African Americans are the only group of immigrants who didn't want to come here. It is saddening to think that their descendants cannot say 'Thank God they took the risk, came here, and laid the foundation for the much better life that I and my family now enjoy' as I have often gratefully said. I'm sure I would have a very different perspective with a background of slavery.

Of course, many Africans have emigrated here deliberately in more recent times.

Who were these Englishmen who prevailed in the wilderness? Separatists (those separated from the Church of England) and religious purists, along with many unaffiliated settlers, went to Plymouth and Massachusetts Bay, and subsequently spread outward to Providence, the Hartford area settlements (New Haven was settled separately), and to what later became New Hampshire, Maine, and Vermont.

The Pilgrims, in Plymouth were the first northern English settlers. They lacked many basic skills (like farming), settled on poor, sandy soil, were lightly financed, and never became a factor beyond the prestige, even adulation, of being first in the North and showing the way.

In the years that followed, better financed settlers, now known as the Puritans, poured into the better lands around Boston and rather rapidly spread in all directions. These people, many of whom came firstly for the freedom to live as God intended, established a religious commonwealth which then denied citizenship to other sects. At their nadir, they executed five Quakers (and flogged many others, both men and women) who persisted in promulgating their faith.

They claimed precedent for their actions in English laws prescribing the same punishment for the return of banished Jesuit priests.

"I thought that the Pilgrims and Puritans were the same; were they different?"

"They were the same in many ways, but there was at least one important difference that was more political than religious. Both groups revered and feared God and viewed the English Government and Church as corrupt. The Pilgrims withdrew (separated) from the English Church and were immediately chastised. Their withdrawal was an affront to and repudiation of the Church. Some emigrated to The Netherlands.

The Puritans remained hopeful that the Government and Church would adopt more Godly practices. They emigrated to New England for many personal reasons but also to establish a society that might serve as a model of righteousness for others, particularly their English brethren, to follow. They were careful not to cross the fine line into separatism and thus escaped the enmity that was directed against the Pilgrims.

And, yet, within twenty years they were emotionally prepared to fight if the Crown attempted to seize their Charter. Although the threat never materialized, it was a very early example of the feelings that would boil into revolution 150 years later."

"What were their "personal reasons?"

"Mostly, the fear of God. Most of the inexplicable events in their lives were believed to be manifestations of the will of God. Sin would likely provoke the wrath of God and that wrath might well strike the innocent along with guilty. If they couldn't convince their English neighbors of the need for a higher level of morality then it might be better to risk the rigors of colonization than to live among incorrigible sinners who might be punished by plague or any of the other epidemics that periodically occurred."

"Wow! That takes some of the luster off their image."

"They definitely had a dark side. Since all might suffer from the sins of a few then the entire community kept its members under surveillance. Harsh penalties were inflicted upon neighbors who were reported to the leaders. Many transgressions were punishable by death, including blasphemy, false witness, and witchcraft. Knowing this, it's easier to see how the Salem witch trials could occur.

Of course, over fifty crimes were punishable by death in England during those same times.

Some of the leaders (especially the very capable John Winthrop) and ministers felt that some leniency was appropriate considering the harshness of the settlers' lives but too much deviation from orthodoxy could get one banished to Rhode Island.[3]"

"And they still thought they were going to heaven?"

"That's a complicated question that I can't adequately answer. Their religion believed in predestination - that everyone was destined for heaven (or not) at birth and the individual couldn't earn his/her way there. There was no sure way to tell who was chosen. However, I suspect that most of the people enduring all the hardships had a good feeling about their chances."

William Penn acquired Pennsylvania for the Quakers in lieu of repayment of a debt owed to his family by the King. The territory had already been sparsely settled for decades. The original settlers were absorbed and the area that is now Delaware was added for administrative reasons in 1682. Delaware had been originally settled by two boatloads of Swedish traders in 1638, absorbed by the Dutch in 1655, and captured by the English in 1664.

Lord Baltimore chartered Maryland as a haven for all religions. Many Catholic settlers came, although they were soon outnumbered and politically disenfranchised. The capital was moved to Annapolis and discriminatory laws were enacted against the Catholics similar to those in England and Ireland.

Probably because of the low population pressure and the humble background of the other settlers, these anti-Catholic laws were not enforced with the vicious zeal of the old countries. Although Catholics were denied access to government and some professions, they were not deprived of their land and could be as financially successful as their neighbors.

It seems as though the logic behind the seeming dichotomy in the treatment of Catholics was institutional. Catholicism was dangerous and must be officially suppressed (perhaps for good reason, from an English perspective), but Catholic neighbors were accepted as individuals, so long as they could accept the blatant discrimination legislated against them.

A practical example of this dichotomy occurred in the early days of the Revolution when it was proposed that a delegation be sent to explore the interest expressed by some of the Catholic French Canadians in joining the rebellion.

Among the five delegates selected were senior statesman Benjamin Franklin (who really thought that he would not survive the rigors of the trip but dutifully went anyway), Charles Carroll, a Catholic, a signer of the Declaration of Independence, and one of the wealthiest landowners in the Colonies, and his cousin, a Jesuit priest.

This obvious pandering to the French was not successful and the expedition was quickly sent back home.

There was little reason for the French Canadians to suffer the pains and risk of rebellion since the recent English conquerors had adopted an enlightened, *laissez-faire* attitude towards them despite their religion.

Conversely, the English colonists to the south had bitterly fought and reviled the French for more than a century.

In the unlikely chance that the rebellion should succeed, Canada would be a junior partner in the new government; a 14th State. It was an easy decision to choose peace and retain their separate identity under the benign British instead of war and an unpredictable union with the formerly antagonistic Americans.

Some books identify Georgia as a colony established for criminals - something of a rehabilitation effort. This is the wrong impression. Georgia was established as a military buffer against the Spanish in what is now Florida by another most capable man who was ahead of his time in many ways - James Edward Oglethorpe.

He had previously conducted a study of the atrocious conditions in England's debtors prisons and many debtors (also English outcasts) joined his colony along with a detachment of Scottish soldiers, some with families.

They were later joined by others including a congregation of European Jews, some of whom had converted to Christianity in Spain to save their lives, emigrated to England, and returned to Judaism.

This congregation later moved north from Georgia to the relative safety of Charleston, South Carolina because if they had been captured by the Spanish they would have been executed as relapsed heretics (in a most unpleasant way).

Chapter 2
Setting the Stage

"Do you have a feel for the early settlers now?"
"They sure were a motley bunch."

"For sure, and that's an important point. Religious zealots in New England, merchants of all nationalities in New York and New Jersey along with residual Dutch and German landowners, Quakers in Pennsylvania, Catholics in Maryland, adventurers in Virginia, plantation owners and small farmers in the Carolinas (many of whom had abandoned their lands in Scotland and Ireland in the face of Church of England opposition to other Protestant sects), and a hodgepodge of settlers in Georgia. But, slowly, they had begun to trade and intermingle."

"And on their way to becoming Americans?"

"Not so you would notice. Regional issues predominated, even to the point of occasional hostilities. It wasn't until the British government began to interfere with all their lives that they realized how much they had in common."

"Another thing. Why did the English settlers in America treat outsiders so much better than they would have been treated in England?"

"Because the strangers had value in a place where there was a big task and too few people to do it. The Old World had been settled for centuries and there was an excess of people, except for the period following the plague, the Black Death, when more than a third of the population died.

An excess population usually leads to social stratification - like the caste system in India. The people in the lower strata become exploited in order to enhance the lives of those above them.

Interestingly, after the plague, the scarcity of laborers led to great strides in the recognition of personal worth in Europe.

The same scarcity existed in early America. A continent was available for settlement and the English colonies needed hands to build farms, establish businesses, fight natives, and resist Spanish and French competition. Any willing and capable hand was valued.

I grew up during World War II. Petty differences were forgotten and we felt like we were part of a single country with a mission. Although some groups experienced discrimination, especially Japanese Americans, the war needs pulled most of us together."

"Then that war did some good?"
"Yes, despite its horrors, a lot of good resulted: to name two gains, the European colonial empires were dissolved, bringing self determination to hundreds of millions of people and the need for a world organization was finally agreed upon and the United Nations was established."

"It's really too bad we don't always see the value in other people."
"The competition for the attractive things in life is strong."

"What happened next? Are we at the exciting part now?"

"War, but not rebellion yet. But given the nature of the colonists and the inflexibility of British colonial policy, rebellion was likely inevitable and if it had failed initially, the unrest probably would have continued to simmer until something changed - another rebellion in another year or a change in colonial policy.

And rebellion was more likely than enlightened administrative change. The British aristocracy was too successful in the present to recognize the potential future benefit from change. For example, an occupying army had to be maintained in Ireland, a country too small for successful rebellion, for centuries because of Britain's inability to construct an acceptable environment. I doubt that it would have been any different in the American colonies.

Let's go on."

The French and Indian War 1756-1763

We have mentioned the French presence in North America before. They were primarily occupied with trading for native furs, missionary endeavors, and some farming. Most of the "settlements" existed to support and defend these activities and were not impressive when compared to those in the English colonies.

But the geographic range of the French settlements was truly impressive as early as the mid 18th century. Up the St Lawrence River to the Great Lakes and down the Mississippi River all the way to New Orleans, they had completely encircled the English.

More importantly, they had staked a claim upon the fertile land across the Appalachian Mountains and into the Ohio Valley. This was the natural direction for American expansion, an expansion that was opposed by the natives and the powers in Paris and London.

But this huge encircling net was severely stretched and militarily weak. And the English colonies had grown in population and strength.

The Seven Years' War was a world wide war among the European colonial powers. The North American segment of that war is known as the French and Indian War. Although there was serious and bloody fighting along the disputed boundary between the French and British colonies, the major victory occurred on the Plains of Abraham at Quebec City where the British forces under Wolfe defeated the French led by Montcalm and Canada soon became British. This victory eliminated one of the most contentious North American issues - influence in the Ohio Valley with its rich farmland and linkage to the Mississippi River commerce.

Interestingly, there was serious debate over what should be given back to the French to induce them to sign the peace treaty and it boiled down to Canada or Guadeloupe, a rich source of sugar.[4] Some on both sides correctly predicted that without the pressure from France, the American Colonies, no longer needing British protection, would eventually strike for their independence.

I wonder if the visionaries would have still been correct if Britain had not precipitated the break by provocative legislation and intransigence when compromise was suggested.

Overall, the war was a great success for Britain.

Colonial militia troops, although subordinate[5], participated alongside British regulars in the defense of the colonies and learned the art of warfare, both formal and frontier style. The militia officers were able to observe the strengths and weaknesses of traditional military tactics and the guerrilla warfare of the natives; more importantly, they learned how to lead and motivate citizen soldiers. They also developed a sense for the limits of these men who were inclined to shoot and run rather than risk their lives in face to face battle. The militia men were individuals, essential to the existence of their families, not military automatons.

The militia officers also learned military administration and the importance of providing for the living and fighting needs of their men.

The war also induced them to form into military companies and stirred the first sparks of nationalism, a sense of something larger than their home town or colony.

A colonial officer named George Washington learned about war (some say he started it) as he led colonial troops attached to General Braddock's army.

The war was costly and left the combatants' treasuries seriously in debt. The British looked for ways to raise revenues.

At this point, it would be well to consider the British colonial master plan. In short, all their colonies had three distinct roles; all other roles were reserved for the home island and the wealthy power brokers there:
- Provide the raw materials for English industry.
- Provide a market for English products.
- Provide the troops and other resources necessary for war.

It was frustrating, therefore, for emigrant, educated, entrepreneurial, Englishmen to find themselves restricted to an essentially agrarian and fishing economy. Not surprisingly, financial opportunity, combined with very little British enforcement capability, resulted in illegal ventures - principally smuggling. The Royal agents were usually easily and openly bribed to overlook the practice but if differences occurred they were apt to be assaulted with impunity.

Things reached an extreme when a British Navy lieutenant, attempting to do his job, ran his schooner, the *Gaspee*, aground while chasing a local smuggler[6] who knew the shallows of Narragansett Bay much better than he did.

That evening, the good citizens of Rhode Island, led by John Brown, the founder of Brown University, overcame the Navy guard and burned the British ship to the waterline.

A British government team sent to find and punish (hang) the perpetrators went home in frustration after months of futile investigation. Only one man, a slave named Aaron Briggs, responded to the reward for testimony. His stories, however, were inconsistent and not credible and of no use.[7]

Who's Boss?

The Seven Year's War was over, the French menace was gone, and the cooperation and military support of the North American colonies was no longer needed by London. So the King and Parliament determined to attend to some housekeeping and the way to do it was to demonstrate their absolute governmental power - and raise some sorely needed revenue at the same time.

Taxes were levied on certain imported goods such as molasses, playing cards, lead, paint, glass, and tea at various times; the goods had to be imported into the colonies since local manufacture was not allowed.

These taxes were modest but the colonists screamed their reaction and the screams were amplified by the rabble-rousing opportunists as well as political visionaries who saw these taxes as the tip of a much larger iceberg. The screams were answered by the strengthening of the British military presence. The colonists, in return, refused to pay the salaries of some of the royal officials and effectively boycotted the taxed products.

After the initial reaction, the question upon the colonists was what to do about the taxes? Formal and informal requests for relief were sent to England. A fitful succession of taxes were tried, rescinded (by a narrow margin), and tried again by Parliament.

The more thoughtful, less emotional, colonial position became "no taxation without representation" implying that the colonists did not dispute their responsibility to contribute to the support the government of the mother country but that they wanted to decide when and how much, perhaps as part of a larger parliamentary prerogative.

At this point, few Americans listened to the radicals who suggested independence, but the idea had been voiced.

Many in England supported compromise - these colonists were, for the most part, freeborn Englishmen, were they not? True, originally some were despised Separatists and others the unwanted dregs of English society but that was 150 years ago and no longer a relevant issue. It was not as if they were dealing with the French, or Irish, or West Indian slaves, or other foreign peoples.

To their everlasting regret, the King and Parliament stood firmly on principle (*Dieu et mon droit*) and rejected the overtures and opportunities for compromise. All the while, they vacillated continually in decreeing and rescinding the various taxes. The majority Tory party dictated a hard line while the minority Whigs urged compromise.

When, a few years later, the English finally came to offer compromise it was no longer an option; they had missed the opportunity.

In the colonies, the pot boiled. Speakers became increasingly inflammatory and the radicals were gaining an audience. Confrontations with Royal authorities and pro-British Loyalists became more frequent.

The colonists had carved successful lives and properties out of the wilderness (over the dead bodies of the natives) and felt personal ownership and the proven ability to overcome obstacles. Further, as we have mentioned before, they were self selected risk takers, people of action who had left the security of an adequate life in Europe to risk, and in many cases lose, their lives to violence and privation in the New World. But, as a society, or rather, as a collection of separate societies, they had overcome the obstacles and were beginning to prosper. The transplants had survived.[8]

With the French threat eliminated, the Spanish threat far away for most, and the rich farm lands to the west now beckoning, the future looked very bright indeed.

"I can hear the heavy music now; the trouble always starts when things look best"

"And this is no exception. You're right; the dramatic scene changed rapidly."

It had to happen somewhere sooner or later and, not surprisingly, it happened in the small city of Boston in the Massachusetts Bay colony (which included the Plymouth Colony, absorbed nearly a century before).

Tea, the currently taxed product, was not being sold because of the boycott against taxed products in the colonies. The East India Tea Company, despite its powerful friends at Court, was losing money as its product sat in London warehouses. Poverty and unrest was on the rise on the Bengal tea plantations. The British government was under pressure to solve these problems. They decided to send the tea to the colonies and demand that it be paid for, tax included, regardless of whether it was resold to the boycotting citizens.

Government response to special interest groups is not a new phenomenon.

The three ships carrying the tea to Boston were not allowed, by the citizens, to land their cargo so they lay at dockside awaiting resolution of the impasse. Similar actions were taken in other colonial cities. The impasse in Boston was decided with finality when a band of disguised men broke into the ships' holds and threw the boxes of tea into the harbor, ruining it.[9]

Boston was rightly (from an English perspective) held accountable and events moved quickly and predictably. Very simply, the loss had to be paid to the last pence by the city. To provide incentive, the government closed the busy port to commerce and put it under martial law.

But they didn't properly gauge the temper of the citizenry.

Undoubtedly, some people cursed the rabble and begged the forgiveness and leniency of the Crown. But the majority dug in and prepared for a long siege. Commerce was conducted out of the neighboring ports, particularly Salem, and the countryside rallied to relieve the hardships of the Bostonians. The people of Massachusetts Bay had overcome worse challenges in days past and had every reason to believe that they would survive this one as well.

The autocratic closing of Boston harbor was a wake-up call to all the colonies. If it could be done to Boston, it could be done to any of them, and most had given the Crown cause. True, the people of Boston had behaved rashly; Britain had told them that they simply had to pay for the tea to right things, and they certainly would not pay without coercion. But many colonies had already pronounced the tea tax illegal, since they had not been represented in the body that imposed it; all of them had resisted British rule to some degree (burning the revenue schooner was a whole lot worse than destroying tea) and, most importantly of all, the Crown had acted autocratically and would not hesitate to do so again.

The fuse had been lit. Militia companies began to reform as in the old days of the French menace and the hardened veterans and their experienced, proven officers began to mold bullets and whet their rusty swords.

Chapter 3
War

Spring of 1775 found the British chafing in their Boston quarters and the rural militias stretching their legs and preparing for the unknown. The townspeople of Boston for the most part were annoyed by the military presence and deeply resentful of the privations from the enforced closure of the port. To be sure, there were other opinions: many made a nice living from the services that they provided to the Army and the individual soldiers. The wealthier were conducting their businesses elsewhere and possibly preferred the security and stability that the military brought with them to the increasing risk of a mob violence that might well target them.

General Gage, the commander, decided that a military exercise would send the proper message to the colonists and the King that he took his assignment seriously.

"I know this part. The British marched out to Concord and started the Revolution."

"True, but you may not know that it wasn't the first sortie out from Boston. The previous September a similar night march to Cambridge had seized the colony's entire store of gunpowder.[10]

Or it could have started on the North Shore in the Beverly-Salem area. They went there almost two months before the famous Concord march."

"Why?"

"The same reason, war materiel; this time cannons."

"Did they fight?"

"Apparently not. The armed minutemen opposed them and unpleasantries were exchanged, but no bullets. The British returned without the cannons.[11]

As you already know, the Concord march had a very different outcome."

Orders were given for Lt Col Smith to march a detachment of infantry on the night of April 18/19 to the western town of Concord where military stores, powder, and shot were to be found and destroyed. There was also the possibility of seizing one or more rebel leaders as well. Smith was to be supported by cavalry officers who would command the roadways and interfere with militia communications.

The British activity was soon known to rebels in Boston who implemented a plan to alert the rural militia.

Who were these militia warriors - some sworn to respond to any emergency on a minute's notice and known to all as the Minutemen?

They were farmers, rural merchants, even a few clergymen, supported by their wives and willing to fight for home, family, and a way of life they deeply treasured and wished to pass on to future generations. Many were descended from the men and women who had seen so much go up in smoke and so many go into the grave, a hundred years before, during the native uprising known as King Philip's War. Later generations had anxiously watched to the north for Indians led by French officers.

More importantly, what were they not?

They were not wild eyed radicals out to change the world; they had a much more parochial vision.

They were not opportunists hoping to profit handsomely from unrestricted commerce and access to the boundless lands to the west, although the stories of the rich Ohio Valley could make a New England farmer, tired of harvesting his annual crop of rocks, dreamy.

They were not visionaries projecting a great empire beginning with the annexation of Canada.

They were not rich smugglers, men with a price on their heads, whose best chance of survival was to rewrite the rules.

Most importantly, they were not suicidal; they had seen the stark realities of frontier warfare and preferred not to be listed as a casualty. Dead men could not harvest the crops and provide for their families, severely wounded men were dead men, and men lacking a limb or two were next to useless. In fact, their preoccupation with survival was the despair of their officers and the comfort of their enemies.

They were not angry killers, swaggering around and hoping for a clear shot at a British soldier - their principal hope was that the soldiers would just go away, the port would reopen, and life could get back to normal.

Finally, they certainly were not political philosophers, dedicated to establishing a new world order based upon equality and the civil rights of all people - yet, that is exactly what they set in motion - a very slow motion, to be sure, but **the great gift from America to the world and to the evolution of mankind.**

These were the men who assembled on Lexington Green April 19th, 1775, in response to messengers from Boston who arrived hours before the British troops.

What was in the collective mind (if such existed) of the militia as they set out to confront and later to annihilate the representatives of the British Crown? They clearly thought themselves to be in the right and that the Crown had acted improperly to impose its will through taxes and the heavy handed closing of Boston to commerce. Certainly, Britain had shown what little regard it had for them and deserved little respect or allegiance in return.

"Wasn't it hard for them to decide to fight the British? Some of their relatives may have been soldiers.
Weren't they afraid?"

"The older settler families had been in the colonies for many generations by 1775. Although some may have maintained contact with British relatives, it is unlikely that many did so. Although they dutifully flew the British flag and acknowledged the Royal Governor, they had become a new people in spirit. Many of their ancestors had emigrated as outcast people with little love between them and the government that they left behind.
The King was not loved. He was descended from a line of German cousins for whom even the English people had little affinity. The Stuart lineage had been an alternative, but their cause died with the charge of the Scottish highland clans at Culloden a generation before.

The colonists must have preferred a peaceful solution to war. They had tried supplications for compromise. But I think that they were not afraid. Death was a much more familiar occurrence in those days and people probably accepted the fact that it happened, that it could come swiftly and with little warning, and that it could come in many forms. Military action was just one of these many forms."

"Why do you say that death was more familiar?"

"Because people mostly died at home, often suddenly or after just a few days' sickness, often with no medical understanding of what had killed them. Most occupations could kill. Childbirth killed. Disease killed, especially children, often many within the same family before it ran its course. Within a generation past, sudden death came from the forest in the form of ravaging 'savages.'

Today, in America, people usually die in a hospital or nursing home for understandable reasons and after a degenerative illness that may have robbed them of their vitality long before their final breath. Death is no longer ever-present or random. A long life, supported by a prudent life style and medical intervention, is the norm.

The colonists had seen much death. Because they were risk takers they did not retreat from life in fear of it; it was just another factor to be recognized.

They had succeeded in the past as a society despite the deaths of so many individuals. They had grown from a few hundred to a population of about 2.5 million by 1775. They had every reason to expect to continue to succeed and to expect casualties as the price of that success."

"But why weren't they more afraid? Britain was the most powerful country in the world."

"They should have been very concerned. We will soon see how badly they misjudged the power of Britain.

But try to look at things from the colonists' very limited viewpoint. They had fought in a war against a European world power (the French), had suffered relatively little, and had been on the winning side. They were used to frontier living; as a last resort an individual could disappear into a frontier where no European army could find him. Finally, they had lived in close enough familiarity with the army in Boston to develop the accompanying contempt.

What they didn't sufficiently appreciate was that the British presence in Boston was but a small garrison. The British Empire was too large to comprehend.

They sensed the vastness of this new land and their own burgeoning population. They knew that Britain could not contain a frontier with a scattering of small forts nor hope to suppress the entire countryside by armed occupation.

Napoleon should have realized that he had no hope in Russia for the same reasons."

Lexington and Concord

The men in Lexington gathered, waited, talked, and wandered about in the quiet darkness. It seemed that the alarm may have been erroneous and many had gone home again before the first martial sounds were heard in the distance at dawn. People, mostly men, scurried about and managed to be in a rough sort of formation in front of the church on the Green to meet the British when they arrived. The colonists were commanded by Captain John Parker who, like so many others, had learned soldiering with Rogers' Rangers in the French and Indian War.

Col Smith, aware of the turmoil in the countryside, had sent word back to Boston that reinforcements might be needed. By this act of prudence, he saved his command from complete annihilation.

The Lexington militia were outnumbered and facing professional soldiers but, amazingly, they held their ground - perhaps because they felt so strongly that *it was their ground*. They were told to drop their muskets and leave by Royal Marine Major John Pitcairn. No one left, and the tension of the confrontation heightened.

Heavily outnumbered, Parker gave the word to withdraw and the militia slowly moved backward. No one dropped his weapon.

Perhaps it was the tension of the moment that was inadvertently transferred to a trigger finger, because a single shot was heard. The British then began firing and the militia responded weakly as their neighbors were falling around them.

Finally, the British officers regained control of their troops, marching order was restored, and the column left for Concord, their destination. The Minutemen had suffered 8 dead and 10 wounded; the British one slightly wounded.

The first blood of the revolution had been shed and there was a score to be evened. It would be paid in full by day's end.

Major Pitcairn would survive the day but would be shot dead in less than two months.

Very likely, the British officers were told to avoid a fight if at all possible before they left Boston. They had failed to control their troops and the dead men of Lexington lay on the Village Green. Martyrs had been created and the "shot heard 'round the world" had found its mark.

The troops resumed their march towards Concord amidst the wild pealing of church bells but without further challenge. The countryside was alive with gathering men while the people of Concord moved as much of their supplies as time allowed. The rebel leaders made their escape.

Upon entering Concord, Col Smith sent detachments into the countryside and to block the North bridge entry to town while the rest of his men began the search for rebel war materiel.

Meanwhile, militiamen were arriving from surrounding towns. Many gathered on the sloping fields below Barrett's farm overlooking the North Bridge over the Concord River, now defended by British regulars. The militiamen milled about, contemplating the actions that they might take. There was no single leader nor any agreed-upon goal, let alone a plan for advancing it. The regulars were tearing the planks off the surface of the bridge, but this was hardly reason to begin battle. The planks could be easily replaced and their removal worked both ways since it would make the further advance of the British just as difficult as the passage of militia.

That the soldiers should proceed no further would have been a goal of the militia if they had formally listed their goals. Actually, they had already done as much as most hoped to do. They had confronted the British force with force, as they had in Salem, and the British had stopped. Now, if the British would just go back to Boston it would be fine with most of them. It was a bit like having a hornets' nest or skunks near your home; you're perfectly happy to just have them leave. Attempting to kill them may produce a less satisfying result.

Meanwhile, the British in Concord had created a rather meager pile of materiel meeting their arbitrary definition of "military" and were preparing to burn it. Had they arrived with more secrecy and with less delay they would have found more rewarding things to destroy.

Two cannons were thrown into a pond and later easily retrieved. The pile was torched, along with a couple of buildings, and the army relaxed as they watched it burn and prepared for a return march to Boston.

A march that would turn into a rout and punish them severely.

The sight of smoke rising from the direction of the center of Concord energized the men on the far slope. It was assumed that the British were burning down the village and this fell within the list of affronts that demanded an immediate reaction.

As if by silent order, they surged towards the bridge which was still passable. The British guards fired a wild volley, hitting four, and began a hasty but orderly retreat towards the town and their comrades. Shots were returned, 12 British dropped, and the militiamen pressed on.

The prostrate casualties in red uniforms and brown homespun testified to the reality that a shooting war had begun.

At the sight of their now running bridge guard, the soldiers in Concord tensed and their officers prepared to form them into a line of defense. But no attack came, only sniping "from behind each fence and farm yard wall" as Longfellow later wrote. Although mostly ineffective, the sniping made their position in town untenable and Col Smith prepared to march back the way they had come, having no reasonable alternative.

The retreat was awful. The sniping was now having an impact and the hot, tired redcoats staggered into Lexington wondering if they would live to go much further - a total reversal of the haughty arrogance of the morning's easy slaughter of the Lexington Minutemen.

Salvation! There were British reinforcements in Lexington - fresh soldiers and cannon that commanded the road to

Concord and seriously intimidated the following militiamen. The reinforcements were under the command of General Percy and they were there in response to Col Smith's earlier appeal.

Smith's detachment rested for an hour and then resumed their tortured march which eventually cost the British nearly 300 troops and all of their hopes for a militarily enforced peace. They settled into Boston and assumed a defensive position while the militia consolidated their hold on the surrounding countryside.

The popular image of Minutemen picking off the marching British with deadly accuracy borne of wilderness training is very wrong. In coming days there would be marksmen worthy of the name, but the men from the Boston area villages were long removed from the forest and the savage. They mostly carried old smoothbore muskets no more accurate than those of the British. More importantly, British flankers protected both sides of the marching column wherever the terrain allowed, forcing the snipers out of accurate range.

No one knows how many of these militiamen assembled along the road back to Boston, but 3,000 is a reasonable estimate. If each of them fired ten times, then 30,000 rounds yielded less than 300 casualties. Not an impressive result.

One anecdote is worth retelling as it portrays the gritty character of the early rebels; the spirit of a people willing to sacrifice everything for principle.

In Menotomy, now Arlington, near Boston, 80 year old Sam Whittemore was banging away at the returning redcoats from behind a stone wall when he heard a noise behind him. It was five British regulars, flankers, who were driving the snipers away from the road and they were coming straight at him. He turned and dropped one with musket fire. Drawing pistols he killed two more and mortally wounded a fourth before he was struck in the head by a musket ball and knocked unconscious. The remaining soldier repeatedly bayoneted and bludgeoned his senseless body.

He was carried to a medical center, treated, and given up for dead.

But dead he was not; in fact, he lived another 18 years.

The man who treated him was a Doctor Tufts from Medford.[12]

After the Concord fiasco, the British hunkered down in Boston and the colonists set up camps all around them. Since the British could be supplied by sea, they were in no danger of being starved out. Neither side could move effectively; the colonists certainly couldn't assault Boston and the British dared not venture out lest they suffer needless casualties and because they could achieve nothing of strategic importance by such sorties.

An important transformation was taking place, however. As volunteers trickled in from other colonies the confrontation was no longer just Massachusetts Bay vs Britain; it was expanding into a colonial war. Also, many other colonies began to debate the problem from an common standpoint, although they were still a long way from declaring independence.

The British government sent three very capable generals to Boston; William Howe, Henry Clinton, and John Burgoyne. The King was not pleased.

Ticonderoga

The fort near the southern terminus of Lake Champlain called Carillon by the French and now Ticonderoga was a nearly meaningless remnant of the French and Indian War. Since there were no longer enemies to fear, it was lightly garrisoned and not very carefully guarded. There was no longer reason for it to have so many cannon except, perhaps, that they had to be stored somewhere and nobody had seen a need to move them to a more useful place.

Ticonderoga was seized by colonials led by Ethan Allen and Benedict Arnold less than one month (May 10, 1775) after the Concord battle. They wanted to forestall any British movements and perhaps advance their own interest in Canada. They eventually captured Montreal and came close to seizing Quebec City and controlling most of Canada, but in the end it was the cannon from Ticonderoga that proved to be the most useful.

Bunker Hill

About two months after Concord, the colonists decided to move closer to the British by fortifying a hill across the Bay in Charlestown. Bunker Hill was originally selected and has retained the title, but Breed's Hill was thought to be better because it was closer, albeit less high, - a shorter cannon shot to Boston. If the immediate British response could have been foreseen, Bunker Hill might have been the safer choice.

The earthen fort was largely built in four hours on the night of June 16/17 and came as a shock to the wakening British. It was an intolerable affront in addition to its possible tactical value as it put Boston within reach of cannon fire.

It was also a British opportunity. The British had every reason to believe that they could defeat the amateur colonial militia in any normal confrontation. The problem was that the colonials usually didn't allow the British to confront them. They sniped from behind shelter, they inflicted casualties, and then they ran. Today, they were willing to fight directly and the chance to butcher them was not to be missed.

The British generals debated countermeasures and decided to attack the colonials directly. An amphibious landing behind them, closing the road off of the Charlestown peninsula was considered and discarded, supposedly for logistical reasons.

"But you don't agree?"

"I suspect a different reason: the landing would have been such an obvious threat that it would have forced the colonials to flee the hill; the ground would have been won but the chance to inflict casualties and demonstrate the superiority of the British forces would have been lost."

"They should have used the best plan."

"'The best plan' depends upon the objectives of the British. What would you have done; what would your objectives have been?"

"To capture the hill so that the Americans couldn't fire cannon balls into Boston?"

"What if you could do more?"

"Like what?"

"Like kill enough rebels to dampen their enthusiasm for rebellion; to give those colonists who opposed rebellion a stronger argument; to send all those farmers home.

Also, to make a favorable impression on the king and the people back in London who wondered why their army wasn't doing something about those damned farmers."

"The book says that an amphibious landing would have taken too long for the boats to get into position; that the tides weren't favorable."

"It took all day anyway."

"So the British weren't just dumb?"

"Far from it. The officers and men were among the best in the British Army. Their battle plan would have been a smashing success, a punishing victory, if the light infantry hadn't been stopped dead, literally, by a bunch of New Hampshire marksmen."

"I think I see what you mean. A boat would be too obvious; too slow and too threatening. The colonials would do a little sniping and then leave. But if the British could spring a trap with battlefield tactics ..."

"That's exactly what they tried. Let's go on."

British ships bombarded the rebels but the earthen wall thrown up by their digging effectively protected them.

With the primary objective of building the fort complete and the British acting aggressively Col William Prescott, the colonial commander, considered what else should be done. This is what any good commander should do, but in this situation it was a profoundly responsible act because the colonial position was not protected from being outflanked on its left and that's exactly how the British generals planned to trap, dislodge, and slaughter their enemy. If they had succeeded in the slaughter, the infant rebellion might have lost its spirit and momentum and died. Very many people already thought that fighting against the British Empire was not a good idea.

The battle of Bunker Hill was one of the pivotal events in the Revolution and the decision to close the gap on the left flank swung it in favor of the colonials.

Decisions were often made by consensus in militia companies; perhaps it was consensus that placed Thomas Knowlton's Connecticut men on the colonial left on the hillside and John Stark's New Hampshire men blocking the beach path from behind an improvised barricade. It should be noted that John Stark was a proven militia leader, having been an officer in Rogers' Rangers, and his men were from the frontier and accomplished marksmen.

"He sounds like the right guy for the job."

"There were none better.

To me, John Stark epitomizes the colonial spirit and the practical competence of the early leaders. He had been a farmer for the past 15 years but easily resumed his military role when the need arose. In addition to capable, his personality also included descriptors such as hard, independent, and uncompromising. Not surprisingly, he was later passed over for a leadership position appropriate to his experience and abilities and so he sat out much of the Revolution. If the Congress wouldn't give him an appropriate commission, he would stay on his farm - unless, of course, the British invaded New Hampshire. That was, in fact, exactly what later happened when he was destined to once again play a key role and advance the colonial cause.

If I were to nominate a "best supporting actor" for the Revolution, it would be John Stark. He was a star playing a cameo role."

General Howe was chosen to direct the British action. He was a capable general with considerable battlefield experience. He knew how to coordinate the use of light and heavy infantry; exactly the mix of troops he had brought with him.

As the heavy infantry began their steady climb up the hill towards the colonial front, hampered by stone walls, boggy earth, and hay, movements were begun against both rebel flanks.

The marines were on the British left and were totally distracted by enfilading fire from the houses of Charlestown. No problem - the major thrust was to be delivered by the British right. The best light infantry in the army, possibly the world, was sent racing along the firm sand on the narrow beach with the intention of encircling the fort and exposing the entire 1000+ colonials to a murderous crossfire. The rebels could fight to the death or surrender, but they would not escape.

John Stark had driven a stake into the ground about 50 yards beyond his barricade and told his men not to fire until the British reached it. The northern woodsmen were then to fire into the massed soldiers. The kill percentage would be much different from that on the Concord road.

Col Stark arranged his men in three lines; just the way they did it when facing the French and Indians; just the way they told the British to do it and were ignored. Three lines solved the problem of slow reloading; a musket could now be fully reloaded in the time it took for the front line to fire, to move to the rear and begin reloading; for the second line to move up and fire, and to then also move to the rear; and for the third line to fire and move. This tactic allowed a continual series of volleys - a very desirable thing when facing crafty savages waiting to charge as soon as all the muskets were empty.

With preparations made, the colonials checked their priming and waited.

The preparations were not wasted. The British advance column, narrowed to about four abreast by the narrow beach, quickly reached the stake and were dropped by the accurate fire. The British officers had expected to take some casualties, but they would then move in with bayonets and sweep away the farmers. The volley was unusually accurate and the writhing bodies interfered with progress, but the British regrouped and came on. Volley after volley took its toll and eventually the pile of casualties approached 100.

This was too much. It was suicidal. There was no reason to think that they wouldn't all be killed, so the officers reluctantly allowed a retreat and Howe's plan was shredded along with the corpses on the beach.
   John Stark, viewing the piled bodies, couldn't resist a bit of rustic humor, commenting that he "had never seen sheep lie so thick in a fold".

   Howe now had two choices - a frontal attack against entrenched defenders or abandonment of the hill to the colonials. The first was certain to be bloody, but the alternative was unthinkable. The first frontal attack took heavy casualties and was unable to drive to within bayonet range. But casualties were to be expected and a second attack was launched. The second had the same result as the first and now things were becoming very serious. The only thing worse than abandoning the field would be to leave the army lying dead upon it.

   Between the British charges, colonial marksmen shot down British officers. As a result, the percentage loss among officers was higher than that of the enlisted troops.

   Howe sent to Boston for the remaining 400 men held in reserve and made a another frontal attack which bravely succeeded in overrunning the embankment despite the colonial fire.
   The simple American excuse has been that the colonials ran out of ammunition.

   "Didn't they?"

   "Certainly they had used a lot but I don't believe that they would have met that last charge with empty muskets. It was probably a combination of things and British valor was one of them."

The colonials retreated rapidly but in reasonably good order while the Connecticut men provided covering fire. When the score was tallied, the British held the field and were able to claim the victory. One source states that they had lost 1,054 out of about 2,200 soldiers. The colonials had lost 440 out of 1,000+.

General Clinton said it all - "A dear bought victory, another such would have ruined us."

Bunker Hill was an important factor in their ruination anyway. The colonials had demonstrated their ability to destroy British soldiers in direct battle. Back home, the doubters were fewer now and the optimists were swaying public opinion. Although there were no defining results, many scored Concord, Ticonderoga, and Bunker Hill as 3 wins, no losses for the colonials.

The British were easy! With perseverance they could be conquered as the wilderness and the French had been conquered.

That all these "wins" came at a time and place chosen by the victors who had the option of disengagement, if necessary, was evidently not an important distinction. It would become very evident very soon.

Bunker Hill was the deadliest action that the experienced General Howe had ever encountered. He knew that he was within one charge of having to abandon the field with all its dead and wounded - most of his officers and half his army. It would have been a crushing blow to Britain's and his own reputations. Although physically unharmed, he was psychologically scarred. He would never again frontally attack entrenched colonials, a reticence that cost Britain the Revolution.

The Continental Congress, largely a debating society since it was not empowered to be much more, was also caught up in the enthusiasm of success. They had seen many of their neighbors trek off to Massachusetts as volunteers and Bunker Hill convinced them that it was time to take a formally united action.

"Hey, we would have killed them all if we hadn't run out of ammunition - right?"

In a burst of pragmatism typical of bright people who do not have the luxury of indulging in private agendas, they made a carefully weighed decision and appointed George Washington as Commander in Chief of their "army". He seemed the best choice available:
- He had military experience; he had been an officer attached to the British army during the French and Indian War. Unlike many of his contemporaries who commanded Rangers and other irregulars, he knew how a formal army operated.
- He wanted the job. He indicated that by wearing his old uniform to the Congress. As he so often demonstrated, he was prepared to put his heart and soul into the venture.
- He was from Virginia, the rich, powerful southern colony. His selection emphasized that this was not simply a regional dispute.
- He was wealthy in both land and goods, diluting the argument that the rebels consisted mostly of poor farmers, city rabble, opportunists, and criminal smugglers.
- Through Masonry, he had connections to many capable and influential men.

It would be many years before the American people fully realized how great a choice the Congress had made. George Washington came to fulfill King George's definition of "the greatest man in the world". It seems that the Congress, a body that made its share of poor decisions, worked diligently and intelligently in selecting Washington - and was lucky as well.

Boston

George Washington took command of his spirited but very unprofessional army and began to form them into an organized force encircling Boston. The stalemate was resumed; the colonials were still not capable of defeating the defenders and the British were decidedly less capable of relieving the siege. Summer turned into fall and fall became winter.

Remember the Ticonderoga cannons? In the depth of winter, Henry Knox, a most unlikely commander of artillery was hauling them over the Berkshire Mountain passes on sledges pulled by oxen. Washington placed them on Dorchester Heights threatening the British garrison. After some negotiation, Howe agreed to evacuate Boston peacefully and did so on March 17, 1776.

A century later when the immigrant Irish wanted permission to celebrate their St Patrick's Day holiday, it was denied - but no one objected to an Evacuation Day celebration - resplendent in green.

A Serious Misjudgment

The rebellion had proceeded very well. The taxes, tax collectors, and many of the British governors had been sternly opposed and eliminated. The British response had led to armed confrontation and the colonials had a virtually unbroken string of successes (an attack on Quebec being the only setback).

The British had evacuated Boston and, except for the garrisons in Canada, had been driven out of North America. The loosely confederated colonies had expelled the mightiest nation on Earth.

On July 4th, the colonies declared their independence. There was no turning back now, no degrees of difference in official opinion; we were unequivocally committed to fighting for our freedom.

"Did the Americans think that they had won the war?"

"I doubt that many were that hopeful, but I expect that many thought that they would be able to continue to beat the British as often as necessary until victory was complete."

"Did everyone now agree?"

"No, and that's an important point! The rebels were firmly in control of matters and already punishing those who opposed them - the 'Loyalists'. Some have said that the colonials were pretty evenly split - 1/3 supporting independence and armed opposition to Britain, 1/3 opposing it, and 1/3 who would have preferred to be left alone.

The third in opposition may be an inflated number as it includes the employees of patrician families who may have unenthusiastically followed their masters' leads.

America already had a growing middle and upper class of relatively wealthy merchants who believed that this disagreement would eventually be resolved diplomatically, as many in England also believed. It just didn't make economic sense. There would be some jousting and then cooler heads would prevail and commerce would again flow.

The Empire had put down rebellions many times before; they knew how to do it; it was part of the business of running an empire.

These richer colonists were divided into all degrees of opinion for or against the revolution, but were of a common mind about the future. The Revolution took a very different and longer course then anyone envisioned in those early days, but the gentry were eventually proven right!

When all was finally resolved, trade between Britain and America again flourished."

"What happened next?"

"'Next' was happening already. The British had sent 11,000 troops (3,000 were German mercenaries) into Canada and were assembling an armada of ships and soldiers at Halifax, Nova Scotia to renew the battle for the colonies when and where they chose. Command of the seas allowed such freedom of movement.

Nobody expected the rebellion to be easy, but most colonists didn't dream how difficult it would be.

A confident euphoria reigned."

Chapter 4
Washington's Hard Lesson

"Oh, oh. I hear that music again. Here comes trouble."

"There were a lot of bad times during the Revolution but this was the scariest because we came the closest to losing much of the army and the momentum for independence.

Do you remember my saying that I thought that if John Stark and his New Hampshire men hadn't destroyed the British light infantry at Bunker Hill, it might have stopped the rebellious movement for a long time? The coming crisis could have done the same."

"Yes; but what do you mean by momentum?"

"In many activities, especially sports, when things are going well everyone catches the spirit and works with focus and energy. Something called teamwork emerges and everyone meshes together. Conversely, when things are going poorly, dissension reigns. People begin to think and act as individuals pulling in all different directions. The wisdom and capability of the leadership is questioned and debated; the same leadership that guided them through the good times. The glass suddenly goes from half full to half empty."

"That means it was never full?"

"Absolutely! As I said before, the colonials had an exaggerated, inaccurate sense of their own military capability because of their small early successes."

"Why were they so wrong?"

"Maybe because the leaders wanted to present a confident image; a mass self deception.

But I think it more likely because they had no experience thinking on a global scale; no sense of empire. They thought that they had fought the French Empire in the forests and had won and the British Empire in Massachusetts Bay and had won, but they were wrong. They had defeated local garrisons of these Empires; all the troops that the Empires had chosen to commit to those places at those times.

The British Empire was spread around the globe. Each location had enough of a military presence to protect business interests, to contain the usual level of local unrest, and to discourage attack from other foreign powers.

For example, the British spice islands were coveted by France and Spain and rebellion in Ireland was endemic. The defeat of the garrison was not usually the end of the struggle; the size of the Empire's response to the problem was the truer predictor of the ultimate outcome."

"Maybe they thought that the British wouldn't want to fight any more."

"Maybe. It was their best hope but a pretty forlorn one. There had been peace since the Seven Years' War and the British troops were not seriously tied up elsewhere. Also, they had to deal decisively with insurrection if they wanted to maintain their image; a weak response would only encourage more trouble elsewhere - local rebellion or foreign predation. I think the colonists' best early hope was for a negotiated settlement, one that gave them parliamentary representation, but the British government was too hung up on its Imperial prerogatives to consider it while there was time; then the Declaration of Independence closed the door on a negotiated solution just as the British were willing to consider it.

Shall we go on?"

"Yep."

"The colonial mood changed abruptly at a place called Brooklyn, on Long Island, near Manhattan."

"I've been there. That's where Aunt Bethy lives."

Brooklyn - The Empire Strikes Back

The British had no intention of sailing away from their North American colonies. The time for tentative measures and local solutions passed with the evacuation of Boston and the Declaration of Independence. The Empire moved swiftly to squelch the revolution decisively. They assembled a naval armada of over 300 ships, 90% of which were troop transports and supply ships, and moved a force of 30,000+ soldiers towards their selected target, the key port of New York.

Washington's army had grown to 28,000 citizen soldiers. Their spirit and dedication was more than equaled by their lack of military experience and the lack of experienced officers to lead them in open battle.

Let them pick the place and the time and they would bury the British in the forest but now they didn't have that advantage - they had to fight wherever the British chose to attack.

The British made camp on Staten Island in New York harbor and prepared for the assault. What factors shaped the upcoming battle?

- New York was a very important port city, the third largest in the British Empire after London and Philadelphia.

Politically, Washington couldn't abandon it without a fight regardless of the odds. The rebels had a win streak going and no one would understand or accept an uncontested surrender of New York.
- Howe had overwhelming naval support and could go anywhere he pleased. Washington had essentially no navy. He did, at least, have a group of men with boat handling ability from coastal Massachusetts, led by General John Glover, which allowed him to cross water to salvation numerous times.
- The British had a slightly larger and vastly more experienced army.

Not knowing the British plans, Washington split his army into five divisions with three of them on the southern tip of Manhattan. One division, under the command of the "Fighting Quaker", Nathaniel Greene of Rhode Island, was placed on Long Island on Brooklyn Heights because if Howe should gain control of the Heights, his cannon could dominate all of lower Manhattan, making the rebel positions untenable.

Unfortunately, Greene fell very ill with a malarial fever and command passed through General Sullivan to General Israel Putnam, the wolf hunter from Connecticut, veteran of the old war and the battle of Bunker Hill.

Putnam knew well how to lead militia in battle but lacked experience in the strategic direction of large groups of men and did not respond well to the British attack which came right at him. Probably Greene's presence wouldn't have changed the outcome, because the British landed 15,000 troops against one third as many rebels, but he probably would have made them pay more dearly for their victory.

Howe played Putnam like the proverbial violin, feinting towards the center, tying down the right, and cleverly outflanking the rebel left. Putnam was forced into a reactive mode and Howe then began to roll over the colonials. It was the seasoned pro with the full repertoire against the gutsy club player; it was no contest.

Washington came over, took direct command and sent for reinforcements because he still hoped to successfully defend New York.

Although Howe outnumbered the rebels 2 to 1, those were the same odds he had at Bunker Hill and he didn't want to relive that experience. Besides, he seemingly had the rebel army trapped, giving him all the time he needed to proceed in a cooly professional manner.

General Howe opted for a slow, carefully engineered siege - when he was in a position to quickly smash a large part of the rebel army and capture its Commander and his staff. He would never again have as good an opportunity because Washington learned a hard lesson and wouldn't make the mistake of risking his army twice.

Howe's psychological scars from Bunker Hill had their effect.

It was worse than hopeless. Washington had to acknowledge the reality that he could not keep Howe out of New York and that he could very well be cut off by the Royal Navy, with the loss of half his army and much of the precious artillery. This loss might have ended the rebellion. If he, too, was captured who would carry things on through the dreary years ahead?

Remember John Glover? Under cover of darkness and a fortuitous fog, his mariners ferried 9,500 soldiers and nearly all the cannon from Brooklyn to Manhattan. Washington had extricated his army and could now begin a fairly orderly retreat.

New York was lost. The British force was overwhelming and it was not within the power of the rebels to stop it. But the army was alive and the new phase of guerrilla warfare could begin.

With the loss of New York went the unrealistic feeling that the spirit, bravery, sacrifice, and purity of the revolution could overcome all adversity. Everyone - Washington, the members of Congress, the volunteers, and the civilian patriots - had to acknowledge that the British military was more powerful, that the colonial winning streak was over, that they must adopt a new strategy of containment and attrition, and that they must be prepared for a long war, at best. The euphoria was gone and the gritty determination that had conquered a wilderness must now maintain their spirits.

However, the new reality protected them against misjudgment in the years ahead.

Ironically, it was now the British military and government who suffered from an unrealistic appraisal of their opponents and they would be the ones to suffer next from misjudgment - a misjudgment that would cost them the Revolution, their American colonies, and 100 million pounds sterling.

Despite all the disappointment, we were introduced, however fleetingly, to the man who was, perhaps, the second most valuable in the rebel military - Nathaniel Greene.

Greene was raised in the Quaker tradition, but supported the belief that the problems between the colonies and Britain could only be resolved by force. He was no longer accepted by his brethren, but was warmly appreciated by Washington and the American cause.

Chapter 5
Hard Times

Washington was chased west and south, losing most of the engagements and spending a dreary and painful winter of 1776-77 at Morristown, New Jersey. The British and their German mercenaries were relatively comfortable in New York, especially General Howe and his lady friend. Despite brilliant symbolic victories in the Trenton, NJ area (again made possible by John Glover), Washington watched his tiny army dissolve.

"At this point, we should take a short break and consider the mood of the main players in our drama."
"Why?"
"Exactly the right question - my point throughout."
"I didn't know it was contagious."
"Even worse; there's no cure once you've caught it."

The patriot farmers and shopkeepers had to accept the fact that the British could not be defeated militarily and driven from the colonies. Quite the opposite, the British could go anywhere they pleased as long as they could be supplied by sea. But they couldn't be everywhere, so most of the territory remained under rebel control. British dominance was a bitter change in outlook for the colonials, but they were practical people and they adapted to the situation. Most importantly, by accepting the new reality they surrendered the expectation that their army could protect them. Therefore, their continued support of the army, the Congress, and the Revolution was not dependent upon military supremacy. They were in this for the long haul and acknowledged that they would suffer along with Washington and his men.

The uncommitted disappeared into their homes and villages and could only be provoked by local events that affected them personally, such as a British incursion into their neighborhood. Probably many were supportive in their hearts but too insecure or wary to risk showing that support openly.

If there was no military action taking place, why leave home to endure cold, sickness, and inadequate food, especially when the pay was worthless "Continental" currency?

The gentry were more convinced than ever that the revolution would fail and that things would soon be back to a sensible "business as usual". Their hope, if they lived outside the areas under British control, was to maintain a low profile and ride out the storm, doing what business they could and avoiding any affront to the rebel fire brands. Failing this, they fled to Canada or England taking whatever they could with them. Most never returned.

Those that remained in Canada became the patriarchs of their adopted country. If one visits communities like St Andrews in New Brunswick, one discovers that those same people who are reviled as traitor Loyalists in American textbooks are the revered ancestors of the Canadian people.

The gentry in New York partied and enjoyed the social stimulation that all those dashing, worldly officers - some with cultured wives - brought to the colonial scene.

The Loyalists were obviously heartened by the British presence and many volunteered to fight. Loyalist regiments were formed and some fought very impressively. Bannistre "Bloody" Tarleton led his legion of "Greens" in the Carolinas throughout most of the war, controlling and terrorizing the countryside and acting as the eyes and ears of the British.

The Loyalists were a large factor in the British plan of conquest; the relatively small percentage that came forward was a serious flaw in that plan.

The King and Parliament were at first gratified by the news from abroad. But as uneventful months passed, they became increasingly frustrated. They had created an overwhelming military machine that could roll over any rebel opponent, but it wasn't rolling over anything because the rebels refused to fight and the army needed to remain connected to its supply lines and couldn't, therefore, pursue the rebels around the countryside.

It was also an expensive military machine; fighting or not, the army needed to be clothed and fed and the rented Germans had to be paid for. The mounting frustration within the government made it vulnerable to risky suggestions.

One of those suggestions was soon to set the stage for the eventual loss of the war and the colonies.

Chapter 6
Burgoyne's Ambitious Plan

General John Burgoyne (Gentleman Johnny) was an experienced officer, an intellectual, a playwright, and a person who had been successful in all that he undertook. There was only one problem - he was not an aristocrat - although he could plainly see that he was more capable than many of those that were called "Sir" and "Lord".

His desire for title provoked him to work hard at finding a way to gain one. Accordingly, he thought longer and harder than his colleagues about how to alleviate the King's frustration with the war's lack of progress. He developed a plan (adopted might be more accurate as it had been discussed before), worked out the details, made it his own, and presented it to the cabinet ministers in London. Presentation followed presentation and finally it was approved; his big chance had come!

The basic plan was to seize the mostly water route that separated New England, the heart of the rebellion, from New York and the rest of the colonies. This route began in

Canada and ran through Lakes Champlain and George and then down the Hudson River to New York City, which the British already held. If the New York Colony was pacified and New England thus separated, the plan said that the rebellion would atrophy and die.

At the first level of detail, the plan called for a coordinated three pronged offensive:
1. Burgoyne would move south from Canada with an army of over 8,000 men comprised of British regulars, German mercenaries, Canadian based Loyalists, and natives. He would drive through to Albany, join forces with his colleagues, and continue to New York City. Not only would he seize the water crossings, but he would make a show of British military power away from the sea, intimidating the rebels and impressing the sachems of the confederacy of the six Iroquois "nations". The destruction of rebel fortresses, troops, and morale was also likely.
2. General Howe would move north from New York along the Hudson, engaging Washington's army as he went. It wasn't absolutely necessary that he make it all the way to Albany as long as he caused the rebel army to concentrate on him and not on Burgoyne.
3. General Barry St Leger would travel up the St Lawrence River to Lake Ontario and then sweep eastward along New York's Mohawk Valley destroying rebel positions, encouraging the closet Loyalists to rise up in his wake, and impressing the reluctant native chiefs with the power of the British military - clearly the side to be on.

"I can tell by your voice that there was trouble."
"Right, again! The plan ended terribly for the British, and the longer term effects were the worst of all. Despite its flaws, it still might have succeeded if, as before, it weren't for some dedicated and capable leaders - Arnold, Stark,

Morgan, a young frontier colonel named Gansevoort - and a lot of brave soldiers."

"What were the flaws? Why weren't they seen by the planners?"

"Well, in fairness, it's always easier to identify flaws by hindsight; all you have to do is to start with the known result and work backwards.

And the details of the plan were not all that clear to a government 3,000 miles away in London and dependent upon irregular, incomplete, biased, anecdotal, and slow information from the colonies."

"Then, who blew it? Burgoyne?"

"The flaws were invisible to the ambitious, confident General who saw a glorious personal future at the end of the road in Albany. I doubt that he even wanted to discuss potential problems; he didn't want his plan threatened by objections. Besides, if he met obstacles, he would overcome them; that's what generals were supposed to do.

Anyway, here are the most egregious of the flaws."

Communications. Once begun, the three elements of the campaign would be operating with little or no current knowledge of each other. In fact, it was closer to "no" than "little".

Reliability. The reliability and military effectiveness of both the natives and the Loyalists in the target areas were unknown and usually assumed to be greater than actual. This miscalculation was due to various factors:
- The pervasive feeling of optimism mentioned earlier.
- The assurances of lobbying Loyalists who wanted to induce the British forces to march in and return them to their homes.
- The presumption that the natives, once recruited, could be relied upon to remain for the duration of the campaign. That they had been recruited by gifts, alcohol, assurances

of plunder, and deceit (despite the counsel of their sachems to remain neutral) was a little known or easily forgotten detail.

Past experience had shown that the natives could not be depended upon to perform with the unquestioning obedience expected from British soldiers, but as long as the booty was good and the casualties light they would remain.

Again, assuming success, no one critically asked "what are the ramifications if things don't go well and the natives desert?" This was not a trivial point, as the natives were a key element of the plan.

Command. Burgoyne wrote a supporting role into the plan for his aristocratic superior, Sir William Howe - a direct, albeit illegitimate, descendent of King George I. Since Howe was given no direct orders from Lord Germain in London, he was free to participate to the degree he wished.

For reasons that we can only guess at, he chose not to involve his command very heavily and to play no personal role at all. One guess at his reluctance is that the plan called for him to fight his way through entrenched rebels and, once again, the nightmare of Bunker Hill dominated him.

It has been said that the soldiers fight the enemy and the officers fight among themselves. That this might explain a part of Howe's indifference to the plan is another tempting speculation.

Strategy. It's difficult to picture a thin line of British troops sealing the long, forested boundary between New England and New York even if they did garrison all the usual river crossings. The line would be too porous to stop individuals, and the flow of supplies was not so great that its interruption would strangle the war effort even if it could be stopped.

Perhaps Burgoyne pictured an uprisen Loyalist and native force doing the actual policing. Also, the British may also have hoped to finally encircle and gain control over the six Iroquois nations who had effectively maintained their sovereignty by first balancing the French against the British and now the Americans against the British. The Iroquois had a remarkably sophisticated government for a people considered to be inferior.

Perhaps the emotional impact upon the other colonies of a severed and isolated New England was another British hope.

Finally, the strategy of creating three widely scattered fronts to separate and absorb the rebel forces had the opposite affect. The three British thrusts, positioned on the perimeter of the rebel forces, could not cooperate.

The Americans, occupying the central position, were able to temporarily reinforce both the west and the north with little risk to their main position. These reinforcements tipped the balance in both places and were crucial to the outcome.

Chapter 7
Ticonderoga Revisited

On June 13, 1777 Burgoyne set his plan into motion. A fresh water armada of ships left St Johns in Canada and proceeded along Lake Champlain uneventfully.

The previous year, the energetic and resourceful Benedict Arnold's locally built fleet contested the waters of Champlain; this year there was no opposition and the British landed just north of Fort Ticonderoga while the Germans circled around to the east. Although outnumbered nearly 3 to 1, the American general, Arthur St Clair, attempted to fortify both the fort and the surrounding hills from which the fort could be threatened by artillery.

Every hill except one, Mount Defiance.

Mount Defiance overlooked all the rebel positions and the Americans had considered placing a garrison upon it. But the American lines were thinly stretched, Mount Defiance was too far away for British musket fire to be a threat, and, most importantly, the Americans convinced themselves that it was too steep to haul artillery to the top.

Things are never perfect and reasonable assumptions and gambles have to be taken under the pressures of time and material limitations; however, not placing a garrison on Mount Defiance was not a good decision.

The British also recognized the commanding position of the Mount; unlike the rebels, they thought that they could haul artillery to its peak. And they did!

They hoped to surprise the rebels with a wakening barrage, but their activity on the Mount was seen, the danger immediately recognized, and the Americans made hasty preparations to evacuate Ticonderoga - and what everyone thought was their best hope of stopping the British.

The British awoke to find the Fort nearly empty and set off after the retreating rebels, overtook and killed some, and scattered the rest into the forest. Precious supplies were lost, troops killed, captured, and scattered, and morale sunk even lower.

Burgoyne had easily overcome the inept rebels and his confidence, plans, and dreams were never brighter. Although they paid a high price, the Americans, in retrospect, set the stage for the future by performing so poorly in the present. If only they could claim that they did it on purpose!

One anecdote underscores the level of American military incompetence and is almost humorous in its futility and absurdity[13] . A heavy cannon was loaded, charged, and pointed at a footbridge leading from Ticonderoga to Fort Independence by the retreating colonists. A team of men were left behind to touch it off when the bridge was filled with advancing British. For a time they were in complete command of the fort. It would be charitable to think that they drank the rum to keep it from falling into enemy hands; perhaps they drank it to fortify themselves for the dangerous assignment ahead; anyway, they passed out and the British crossed safely.

Somewhat later, a curious native attached to the British force touched off the cannon and belatedly blasted the bridge.

Burgoyne undoubtedly concluded that the easy rout of the garrison at Ticonderoga was entirely due to the superiority of British military force and skill, under a very capable commander. If he had been truly superior in judgment he would have considered that:
- Ticonderoga was probably untenable; in fact, had the siege been prolonged the Americans would have been completely surrounded and entirely killed or captured. They would have inflicted casualties in the process but the outcome would have been the same - the fort would have fallen and the garrison with it.
- The Americans were outnumbered 3 to 1 with no hope of effective relief from Washington.
- His army was now further than ever from its source of supply and there was little forage available.

There were good reasons for the British to worry that things might not continue to be so easy, but they were immersed in confident euphoria. If this had all been part of a masterful American scam, it had succeeded brilliantly. The mark was now completely set up and now the Americans proceeded to make exactly the right moves.

"Wow! things looked really bad."
"They were at nearly dead bottom, but now proceeded to gradually get better. I wish I could think that the Americans understood, even stage managed, the entire affair. Actually, they took a number of separate steps, all in the right direction."

A Walk Through the Forest

Burgoyne had planned to take the usual route from Ticonderoga to Fort Edward, sailing south through Lake George and traveling the rest of the way on a well worn trail. But part of his army had chased the retreating rebels far into the forest and were now at Skenesboro, not far from Fort Ann which was 3/4 of the way to Fort Edward.

But there was no road capable of bearing his great train the rest of the way - an artillery and supply train that also included wagons full of choice wines and other requisite delectables not otherwise found in the wilderness, plus female companions; spouses and otherwise.

It did not seem sensible to travel back to Fort Ti and back down the originally planned track, a trip of more than 60 miles, when they were only 20 miles from Fort Edward. Burgoyne would cut a road through the forest. He had overwhelming military strength and natives to scour the forest and discourage snipers; he had nothing to fear. The short cut made sense.

It was a bad decision. Although the Americans couldn't attack him, they harassed him so effectively that it took weeks to complete the road.

The British, straining mightily to clear the giant trees that the rebels had dropped across their path could, in the stillness, hear the sound of axes and the crashing of trees in the distance.

Chapter 8
Trouble in the West

Leaving Burgoyne engaged in road construction, let's turn our attention to another phase of his master plan - General St Leger's punitive action intended to defeat and intimidate the rebels, many of Dutch and German descent, in Western New York.

He planned to land at Oswego on the eastern shore of Lake Ontario and drive eastward to rendezvous with Burgoyne in Albany, having swept the Mohawk Valley of rebel control and placed it under the command of resurgent Loyalists. His army consisted of about 800 soldiers and Loyalists and another 800 native mercenaries. These "Indian" mercenaries felt no loyalty and fought mostly for the rewards of war, although the British also promised to put a brake on the expansion of the colonists into the western lands in return for their support. Unlike the German mercenaries, they were freeborn individuals, not serfs or men bound by enlistment, and could leave, as we shall soon see, any time they chose - much to the chagrin of their employers.

Things went smoothly until the British reached Fort Stanwix, a refurbished old log fort about 1/4 of the way to

Albany. It was garrisoned by about 750 Continentals led by a young Colonel of Dutch descent, Peter Gansevoort; and it was provisioned for a long siege.

St Leger demanded surrender, bluntly referring to the uncontrollable wrath of the natives in battle. Gansevoort had no intention of surrendering, the natives notwithstanding. Familiarity at least breeds objectivity and these frontier people had long prevailed despite the continual presence of natives and the potential for violence.

I suspect that the image of rampaging natives was less vivid for the colonials than it was for the British, many of whom knew them by reputation only.

St Leger established camp on one side of the fort, sent the natives to their own encampment, and prepared to lay siege. One problem quickly became apparent - the lightweight cannons that he chose for speedy travel couldn't damage the fort!

Meanwhile, the local Dutch militia colonel Nicolas Herkimer had heard of the invasion and had sent out a call to arms. He quickly assembled over 800 men of the Tryon County militia and marched towards the Fort, bringing more supplies. St Leger received word of his approach and sent the natives and some Loyalists out to intercept the militia. The ambush was was sprung and might have resulted in a bloody massacre of the Americans had they not reacted well and fought back. In a vicious hand to hand battle, hundreds were killed on both sides. The natives could claim success as the relief column was forced to retreat but they had paid a high price.

As a ratio of casualties to the combatants involved, this was the bloodiest battle of the Revolution.

Meanwhile, when he heard of the approaching militia, Col Gansevoort boldly sent a party from the undermanned fort to guide them in. Although the militia relief column was ambushed before it could make contact, the Americans from the fort discovered the native encampment and leveled it, destroying all that the natives had brought with them as well as their spoils of war.

When the weary and bloodied natives returned and found the remains of their camp they held a council which, I would guess, concluded with (roughly translated) " #%*! this".

Remember the advantage that the Americans had from the British decision to attack them from the perimeter? Now was an opportunity and the centrally located American General Philip Schuyler boldly sent 900 of his 4,500 men racing westward under the command of the dashing Benedict Arnold, his only general willing to undertake the mission.

As they approached Fort Stanwix Arnold sent messengers ahead who greatly exaggerated the colonists' strength. The ruse worked. The natives, already losers, decided that it was time to harvest the crops, or whatever, and left for home. St Leger (who has been described as apart from his men and usually drunk), deprived of his natives and facing what he believed to be an overwhelming force, led the disorganized retreat quickly back to Oswego and thence to Canada.

The natives took out their wrath and disappointment on any fleeing Loyalists they chanced upon - and took their scalps also.

Phase two of Burgoyne's master plan was over, utterly defeated by dogged and clever frontier tactics.

And remember the communications problem? Nobody got word of the outcome to Burgoyne for too long a time.

As a footnote, the ability of Col Herkimer to assemble a force of 800 capable, armed men in a very short time exemplified an American advantage throughout the war. The British could never be sure of their enemy's strength despite continual efforts to do so. The volunteer militia men were not as useful as trained soldiers but the mere presence of hundreds or thousands of additional muskets was upsetting. Besides, they came out of dedication, they could shoot straight, and they brought their own weapons, clothes, and food with them.

Chapter 9
A Promise Kept - Bennington

When he was passed over for an appropriate commission in the Continental Army, the extremely capable but difficult John Stark went back to his farm. But he promised that he would fight again if the British ever invaded New Hampshire. That included the wilderness known as the New Hampshire Grants, now the state of Vermont.

By August 1777, Burgoyne had finally cut his way through to Fort Edward and was again moving southward with Albany in the distance. However, the rebels had stripped the land of forage and fresh livestock, especially horses. Burgoyne suggested that Lt Col Friedrich Baum and his German Brunswickers might search for horses, forage, and other war materiel in the New Hampshire Grants, a region supposedly lightly defended.

Baum set out for Bennington with a force of about 300 Germans, 300 Loyalists, 100 natives, and a few British soldiers.

Unfortunately, contrary to his information, the area was not devoid of defenders - the formidable John Stark was headed in the same direction with an army of about 1,500 men recruited by, and answering to, the State of New Hampshire. Along the way Stark encountered some of the survivors of Ticonderoga, the men who had escaped into the forest, under the command of his friend Seth Warner.

Col Baum, recognizing the danger of the situation, sent for reinforcements and set up three encampments - German, Loyalist and British, and native.

Stark developed a brilliant but demanding game plan. He split his army into four encircling columns and personally led the remaining column in a smashing drive against the center. The timing and coordination of the plan would have challenged the best professionals; Stark achieved it perfectly with militia. The encircling movement was so deceptive that Baum actually thought that one column was local Loyalists coming to his aid until they fired into his midst[14].

Now the shoe was on the other foot and it was the natives, Loyalists, and British who fled into the forest for salvation. The Germans fought bravely but they, too, eventually were running in terror through the trees with the body of Col Baum left lying behind. The ecstatic frontiersmen chased the survivors, cutting them down as they ran, and nearly ran into the German relief column under Lt Col Heinrich Breymann.

With fortuitous timing, Seth Warner appeared with fresh troops and held off the Germans while Stark regrouped. A second tough battle sent more Germans in retreat and the bloody survivors of Fort Ti had a measure of sweet revenge.

Burgoyne lost over 900 men as well as many of his natives who left promptly to attend to the fall harvest; the Americans had 30 killed and 40 wounded.

Once again, when allowed to dictate the place and style of fight the Americans showed their mastery. The militia might not be willing to face British troops in massed battles, but they were magnificent in their own element.

John Stark continued to lead the Army of New Hampshire.

One anecdote paints a picture of the confusion and fluidity that surrounded the German/British forces. Wishing detailed information about the enemy defenses, Stark sent frontiersmen pretending to be Loyalist volunteers into the enemy camps. After wandering around and noting everything, they returned to Stark with the best of information. The effectiveness of this ploy was probably aided by the language barrier; the Germans couldn't even start to interrogate the newcomers.

Chapter 10
The Most Important Battle - Saratoga

"Did General Burgoyne stop now?"
"Certainly not."

"Did he go back to Canada?"
"No. Far from it. Burgoyne was troubled by the loss of the men he sent to Bennington but maybe he wrote it off as the fortunes of war in the wilderness. He, however, was safely encamped with his indomitable army and still on track for Albany, fame, and title."

More bad news, however, came quickly:

- General St Leger had been stopped and forced back to Canada. He would not be in Albany.

- General Howe had sailed south to capture Philadelphia. He would not be in Albany either. Howe did allow General Clinton, whose chief responsibility was to hold New York City, to attack up the Hudson.

As usual, the operation was professionally planned and executed and the British succeeded in capturing forts, cannon, and rebels all the way to, but not including, West Point. A feint sent Israel Putnam's force of 1,500 defenders into retreat and out of the picture.

However, Clinton was at the end of his limited men and resources and withdrew to the City with a note to Burgoyne that he hoped that he had been of some service. It was a professional performance but it hadn't helped a bit.

- Jane McCrea was murdered and scalped by Burgoyne's natives. Burgoyne had previously threatened to unleash native savagery and this almost accidental event was widely publicized by the Americans as proof of British inhumanity.

Native savagery was a visceral issue, awakening responses that had been bred into generations of colonists, and angry volunteers again began to pour in, swelling the American ranks to 7,000 and outnumbering Burgoyne's army for the first time. Once again, a British general couldn't depend upon the last count of the numbers opposing him.

That Jane McCrea's death could have been parlayed into a public relations bonanza for the Americans was ludicrous. Jane was a Loyalist, engaged to a Loyalist officer. By one of many accounts she was killed in a crossfire among arguing natives. Her long, beautiful hair was too tempting a prize and the displayed scalp became a powerful symbol in arousing the emotions of people who would have reviled her if they had known more about her and she were still alive.

General Philip Schuyler, who had borne the burden of resisting the Burgoyne campaign was replaced by General Horatio Gates just as things began to turn for the better. Lucky timing; Gates knew how to be a general, but was dull in thought in action. Although not a good choice, he was fortunate to have capable and energetic people around him.

Later, he would prove a disgrace to himself and the army.

The Americans, again able to transfer key people to where they were needed, established a strong position on Bemis Heights overlooking the Hudson and the only road south to Albany. Col Thaddeus Kosciuszko engineered the artillery positions which threatened to destroy anyone or anything passing beneath their muzzles. Benedict Arnold was there, newly back from the success at Fort Stanwix, and Daniel Morgan, the old wagon master, with his Virginia and Pennsylvania frontiersmen - armed with the rifles that could kill effectively at distances far beyond the range of the British smooth bore Brown Bess muskets.

The biggest threat to the American position lay inland from the River, on the high ground to the west where British artillery could blow the rebels away. Arnold saw this and urged a preemptive strike against Burgoyne. "Granny" Gates preferred to wait and so they did.

Eventually, Arnold's urgings, his battlefield fame, and his anger over what he believed to be deliberate omissions of his exploits wore so thin that Gates removed him from a command position, exacerbating the animosity between the two men.

The parallel between Arnold in 1777 and General Patton in the 1940s is remarkable. Both were the best battlefield generals in the army, yet both were ultimately sidelined due to personality clashes with their superiors. In Arnold's case the cause is probably due mostly to Gates' inadequacies.

A more effective use of this sort of talent should be possible.

Burgoyne, experienced general that he was, saw the opportunity on the high ground to the west. If he could seize it, the Ticonderoga story would be replayed, the rebels dislodged, their artillery destroyed, and the march to Albany resumed. The intervening heavily wooded ground was a mystery, however, so he set out on September 19th to feel out the rebel position. Gates made no response, but Arnold, still with a command at that time, bullied him into allowing an American counter advance.

The British advance was divided into two fronts with Burgoyne in the center and the brilliant Scottish General, Simon Fraser, on the right searching for a way through the forest and behind the Americans. Arnold and Burgoyne came upon the cleared land around Freeman's farm and sighted each other for the first time.

Morgan's riflemen opened fire immediately and began picking off the enemy, with emphasis upon officers. It was a turkey shoot, a delightful way to wage war.

Frustrated by the continuing loss of men all around them, the British charged to close the distance. Arnold responded by also moving forward with his Continentals and a brisk fire fight ensued. The British wavered and Arnold asked Gates for reinforcements, saying that he could completely destroy the enemy. The response was a conservative "No".

Baron von Riedesel marched his Germans onto the battlefield and the British were able to extricate themselves in good order.

The British losses were significant but not fatal. They had suffered about 600 casualties, with a disproportionate number of officers who were dropped by rifle fire, to about 300 casualties for the Americans.

Except for the dead men, not much had changed. The Americans were still sitting behind their cannons on the

Heights and the British, although they had advanced their line somewhat, were back in camp without good knowledge of the rebel positions, and unable to continue their march to Albany.

The End Game

Burgoyne knew he had to do something and intended to attack the rebel lines again immediately. Then the communiqué arrived from Clinton telling of his plan to fight his way north from the City. This changed everything. Burgoyne was no longer totally alone. He postponed making plans until he knew more of Clinton's progress.

Nearly a month passed. Clinton had not even begun when he sent his message to Burgoyne; then he awaited reinforcements and had, by now, just barely started. Burgoyne's supplies were running short, the leaves were changing color but they still completely hid the rebel strength and positions, the days were becoming shorter and colder, and it was a long way back to Canada.

The British officers were worried; some counseled retreat, but Burgoyne still looked southward to fame. It was finally decided on October 7th that a scouting expedition might prove useful, the sort of operation that could be best done by a picked force of about 100 men.

But Burgoyne demurred, possibly because he had an unspoken hope. He had so often seen the rebels perform poorly in the field; he had seen them break and run when pressed. Why not take enough troops so that if fortune provided an opportunity he would be able to exploit it?

So a "scouting" expedition of 1,500 mostly British and Germans set out, accompanied by cannon. Simon Fraser led and Burgoyne accompanied the party.

Stealthy, it was not.

The plan was simple. They would move inland and then turn south, hopefully outflanking the rebels and collapsing the defense.

Eventually, the British came to a farm clearing and stopped to rest and reconnoiter. Even from the top of a small building they could see nothing but forest in all directions beyond the field. The scouting expedition was over; they should have returned to camp promptly. But it really wasn't just about scouting and they were already exchanging fire with rebel pickets; Burgoyne had the engagement that he wanted.

Von Riedesel, who had seen a lot of battles, was uncomfortable. Both of the British flanks adjoined the forest and the rebels were at their best in that kind of fighting.

And remember the problem of accurate count? Volunteers still kept coming and some estimates place Gates' army now up 5,000 more to a total of 12,000 men. If this is close to true, the British scouting party was theoretically outnumbered 8 to 1.

The British had seen nothing of the rebels, but they had been watched continuously. At the sound of musket fire, Gates sent out his troops - Morgan, of course, and Henry Dearborn through the forest against the British right and Enoch Poor through the forest on the British left - exactly as von Riedesel had feared. Ebenezer Learned prepared to lead his brigade of Continentals across the open against the Germans in the center.

The Americans moved quickly through the forest and actually outflanked the British who had hoped to do the same to them. They moved easily over the rough terrain and Morgan and Dearborn came screaming over a ridge and through the woods, surprising their enemies as Poor's men fired from behind the trees on the opposite side.

British artillery answered back but couldn't effectively penetrate the forest cover. It must have resembled a giant pinball game with the cannon balls ricocheting off the forest trees.

Both British flanks staggered while the Germans bravely held in the center. Fraser rallied and steadied his troops and they responded well.

It was at this pivotal point that Daniel Morgan turned to renowned marksman and Indian fighter Timothy Murphy, pointed to General Simon Fraser, and is reputed to have said "I have great respect for that man, but he has to go. Take him!"

Murphy took his double barreled rifle into the lower branches of a tree in order to see above the blue smoke hanging over the battlefield and took aim at his target, some 200 yards away.

There is a enough delay when firing a flintlock weapon, between pulling the trigger and the discharge, for an active target to move away. Accordingly, both of Murphy's shots missed the energetic general. Tim reloaded and put the third shot squarely into Fraser's stomach.

He emptied the other barrel into Fraser's aide-de-camp, Sir Francis Clerke[15], killing him instantly.

In those days, a body wound was usually fatal; the only question was whether the wounded person died mercifully quickly or in extended agony. It was all day and all night before Simon Fraser died, probably from sepsis.

A gentleman to the end, one of his last utterances was to the Baroness von Riedesel; he apologized for disturbing the sleep of her and her three young daughters with his cries of pain.

Fraser's loss seemed to take the heart out of the British (or maybe it was his constant pumping that had been keeping them up) and they wavered.

At the same time, another incredible event was unfolding. Benedict Arnold borrowed a horse and rode toward the battle. He was a general without troops to lead and reportedly had been drinking but he charged into the fray like a wild man, totally oblivious to his own danger. Some of the Connecticut men recognized him and cheered. He called to them to follow him and he led a furious charge. The brave German line had to withdraw and, with Fraser now down, so did the British.

Burgoyne's men had prepared two log barricades, called redoubts, and they ran behind these and stopped the Americans. But Arnold could not be stopped for long. The hard charging Americans encircled one redoubt and the Germans had three choices - die, surrender, or run. Each soldier made his choice and the redoubt fell.

As they were overrunning the second redoubt, Arnold's luck finally ended. His bad leg was wounded again and then broken when his horse was shot and fell upon it; he had to be carried from the field.

The Americans had won another huge victory. The British had lost another 600 men (to the Americans' 150), including two generals, and the Americans had captured the high ground overlooking Burgoyne's main camp. The British position had become desperate but, for the moment, both sides withdrew to catch their breath and look to their dead and wounded although most of the British dead (and soon to be dead) were left lying on the field. Wolves howled throughout the night as they fed upon the bodies.

There has been endless speculation over what would have happened if Arnold had not been wounded. Certainly, he would have wanted to chase the fleeing British into the Hudson and the men would have followed him anywhere. But did they have enough energy left to fight another battle?

Might they have thrown away their great gains by sacrificing themselves needlessly? Nearly 4,000 fresh reserves were waiting to defend the British camp.

Interesting speculation - but Gates was no Arnold and he stopped the offensive, rightly pleased with the results of the day.

Burgoyne, for the first time, lacked decisiveness and confidence. With the concurrence of his general staff, they began a short retreat northward, then stopped and opened negotiations with Gates on terms of surrender.

Burgoyne still hoped that Clinton would march in, driving the rebels from Bemis Heights, and reinforce him at any moment.

But time passed and eventually Burgoyne suggested that his army be allowed to return to England, each man having given his promise that he would not fight again in the Revolution. Gates eventually approved the proposal without reservation.[16]

Accordingly, the British surrendered their Northern Army.

"Why did Gates let him go? The Americans could have killed them all from the forest if they tried to retreat. They couldn't ever get back to Canada now!"

"I don't know. Given Gates' reputation for timidity, it's easy to conclude that even then he still feared the risk of battle with Burgoyne and was willing to accept almost any alternative. Remember, he hadn't been close to the battlefield; he hadn't actually seen how thoroughly the Americans had dominated. Also, he knew that the British had armies to both the north and south of him; maybe he feared a rescue mission and felt pressure to end things quickly.

I'm sure that Benedict Arnold would have urged a different sort of end to the issue if he hadn't been busy arguing with the surgeons who felt that amputation of his leg was the only sane choice.

The loss of Arnold may also, begrudgingly, have affected Gates' decision. In his heart he must have known that he had lost an irreplaceable officer.

The paroling of prisoners was not uncommon in those days. However, you'll be pleased to learn that Congress negated the agreement by attaching unacceptable conditions and Burgoyne's army spent the rest of the war in prisoner of war camps.

However, considering Britain's record of perfidy in treaty situations, it's no more than they deserved and, perhaps, expected.

After eventually reaching Virginia via Massachusetts, the British and German prisoners were treated vastly better than the British treated rebel prisoners.

Interestingly, nearly half the German prisoners disappeared. They didn't die. Most walked away and were accepted into German immigrant communities in western Pennsylvania and New York - an eighteenth century version of the underground railroad.

The Americans didn't seem to mind; instead of consuming food, they were growing it, some destined for rebel stomachs."

"Burgoyne was pretty stupid. He didn't have to lose the army. He could have gone back to Canada."

"He certainly could have tried; but it was more blindness than stupidity. I believe that it never occurred to him that he could lose everything until it was too late. He had outmaneuvered and defeated the rebels so easily on so many occasions that he was understandably slow to sense how much things had changed.

And consider this: if you take Arnold out of the picture, the last battle ends with the scouting expedition returning in an orderly manner to camp, still able to return to Canada or gamble on fighting its way southward.

Hindsight obfuscates as well as it clarifies. We can't imagine any other outcome at Saratoga now, but I doubt that the Americans who were there felt the same. They had been beaten and forced back by the British continuously. They thought that they could hold at Fort Ti and saw those hopes easily and totally smashed. They had no great respect for Gates.

Perhaps, tellingly, John Stark withdrew his New Hampshire men from Saratoga on the eve of the first battle. His reason was technically valid - their enlistments had expired. This was consistent with his strict adherence to principles and to all that New Hampshire had commissioned him to do; it was all that the Colony had committed to pay for.

But it was not in keeping with his patriotism and there surely must have been ways to have approved extended enlistments. He couldn't know that Burgoyne was about to attack but he must have known that tensions were building."

"Then why did he leave?"

"I think because he had no confidence that Gates would win and he didn't want to induce his friends to expose themselves any longer. He was not one to fear a fight that he thought he could win, but perhaps he feared that they would be used up foolishly, or surrendered, by Gates. Remember, his neighbors had been shot up pretty badly in the forests fleeing from Fort Ticonderoga.

Returning to the British for a moment, it has been suggested that the government in London saw Burgoyne's plan as risky but let him go ahead anyway. I can imagine something like 'Give the cocky commoner a chance; he may just pull it off; and we certainly won't order Lord Howe to subordinate himself to the plan.' Besides, with the threat of another American invasion of Canada gone, the Northern Army was expendable and the Germans might as well earn their pay.

If that was the British thinking they should not have been surprised that the plan's objective was not met and that heavy casualties had occurred, but they must have been very troubled by the loss of the entire army and the aftermath of the debacle."

"What aftermath?"

"Ah, the biggest question of all; we'll go right into it. In many respects the aftermath was more important than the victory.

But first, one final irony: the British evacuated Philadelphia the next year! The prize of the campaign that had arguably cost them the Northern Army and which then began the chain of events that cost them the war proved to be more of a burden than a prize.

Some think they were afraid that the French fleet might cut off their access to Delaware Bay - which is exactly what happened in Chesapeake Bay three years later!"

Chapter 11
World War

Benjamin Franklin headed a delegation in France for the purpose of securing support for the Revolution. He was a remarkable, self-made man, a scientist and natural philosopher, who even more remarkably was appreciated and honored in his own time. Had he been younger, he certainly would have been one of the eminent leaders of the new country. He was a man of humble birth who grew to his full and immense potential in the free air of the New World. It was as if America had grown him for the purpose of bettering that World.

His delegation had succeeded in eliciting covert financial backing from both France and Spain, but were far from their ultimate goal of bringing France openly into the war on the American side. France was willing to foment trouble for Britain by supporting those who were willing to rise up in arms; but they were less willing to risk their own troops and a costly war in support of a chancy rebellion.

England and France were competitors in a world where warfare was an acknowledged diplomatic tactic. Both sides maintained large military organizations for the purpose of gaining and protecting lucrative overseas colonies. Wars were periodically fought, territories captured and lost, and then treaties drawn to define the new order.

"We've learned about the Middle Ages and the Vikings and Ghengis Khan and all violence of those times. I'm glad that I didn't live then."

"It probably would have been a short life.
We can shake our heads and smile at those sanguinary times but, sadly, not all that much has really changed. Warfare and personal violence are still rampant in human society. We have been free of large scale violence for 50 years because it has ceased to be profitable for the winner. Coming in first in a nuclear war would make one more of a survivor (for how long?) than a winner and everyone would lose much more than they could hope to gain. The "balance of terror" and not the growth of morality has been the real champion of reduced violence over the past 50 years.

And yet there are hopeful signs. Not long ago, a nominally Christian coalition bombed a Christian country (Serbia) on behalf of a persecuted Moslem minority; in my mind, an historical watershed."

Long ago France and, later, Germany supported the cause of freedom in Ireland; certainly not because they espoused freedom for the common people, or because they particularly cared who ruled Ireland, or because they really thought that the Irish had the strength to oust Britain. They supported the Irish because putting down rebellions tied up the British military, cost money, and disrupted commerce from that colony.

There was no concept of International law to discourage warfare, no moral or religious high ground for pacifists. In fact, the religious communities were also competitors. Both British and French troops, the former loyal to the Church of England and latter loyal to the Pope were assured that they were fighting a holy fight against minions of the dark side.

When the American couriers arrived in France, Franklin immediately inquired as to whether Philadelphia had fallen to the British. When his question was answered in the affirmative, the old diplomat slumped over from the weight of the implications.

"But wouldn't you like to hear the rest of the news?" "Saratoga." "The surrender of the Northern Army." Glee best describes the rest of the conversation.

The news was quickly communicated up the French chain of command, and after appropriate consideration and confirmation, France decided to recognize the rebel government of the United States and was automatically at war with Britain.

The effect and implications were immense. The Americans had a world class ally and Britain's colonial insurrection had bloomed overnight into a world war.

Prior to French recognition, the American Revolution was geographically constrained. Britain could send as many troops as she wished into the colonies and conduct the war as severely as she thought best. The Americans could not attack Britain or any of the other British colonies; they could not even attack Canada meaningfully.

After the French recognition, the entire British Empire was up for grabs, especially the extremely profitable Spice Islands in the Caribbean. Having played the military card, France was free to take what she could from a Britain bogged down in a war of attrition in America. It was even conceivable that the British home islands might be invaded[17] .

"Did the French capture British colonies?"

"Much fighting, mostly naval, occurred and territories changed hands. We won't discuss it here because our story is about America; but, as you will soon see, it forced the American war zone further south so that the British fleet could support combat theaters in both North America and the Caribbean.

For all the wrong reasons, Burgoyne achieved a parody of his plan - New England was no longer the center of the rebellion."

Burgoyne's surrender at Saratoga was the pivotal event of the Revolution. From that day forward events moved slowly, albeit sporadically, towards victory for the Americans. The second battle of Saratoga at Barber's wheat field was the pivotal day. The pivotal instant occurred when the bullet tore into General Fraser.

Chapter 12
The Enigma of Benedict Arnold

"Remember Benedict Arnold? Before we go on I'd like to think about this complex man for a moment."

"OK. But why?"

"Because he was a great hero who then made the worst and most outrageous decision in American history. Why he did it is still somewhat a mystery. And you know how I like problems and mysteries."

"Wasn't he the traitor?"

"In a word, yes. And also our greatest and most successful battlefield general.

After enduring great dangers and hardships (including two battlefield wounds) and nearly giving his life for the American cause, he changed his mind and joined the British side.

Simply changing his mind would have been hard enough to understand, but he went all the way and certainly did become a traitor, trying to betray the American defenses at

West Point, which would have opened up the Hudson River to British naval control."

"Why would he do a stupid thing like that?"
"Why, indeed! He certainly had a reason and he didn't think it was stupid. A lot of people have studied and guessed about what was in his mind, but no one knows for sure."
"What do you think?"
"OK; what do I think?"

Benedict Arnold was a pharmacist and merchant in New Haven in the colony of Connecticut. New Haven had been settled separately from the northern villages of Hartford, Windsor, and Wethersfield and was later reluctantly joined with them by British fiat.

Arnold was of old stock, the descendant of a Rhode Island governor, but had to rely on his energy and intelligence to make his own career. A troublesome youth, he had settled down to a town and sea based business that is said to have included the lucrative pursuit of smuggling. Like so many others, he saw a little of military life in the French and Indian War.

He had set off to capture Fort Ticonderoga with Connecticut men when he heard that Ethan Allen was ahead of him with the same plan. He raced ahead of his troops and was, at least, able to say that he participated.

He was recommended for a commission in the new army by no less than George Washington.

He marched and paddled an invasion force across what is now Maine and Quebec in winter only to be wounded and fail in the capture of the Quebec City. This little remembered march was a tribute to his drive and his men's endurance. He commanded the small American force holding Montreal until the City became untenable.

He built a small fleet from scratch on Lake Champlain in 1776 and delayed a much stronger British fleet long enough to force them to retreat before a much more formidable force - winter.

He was the only general willing to lead the reinforcements to the relief of Fort Stanwix. His clever deception sent the British scurrying back to Canada.

He was the most notable hero in the American victory at Saratoga, was wounded, and nearly died twice as he fought to avoid the amputation of his his badly damaged leg - the same leg that was wounded at Quebec.

After his great effort at Saratoga, he lay in agony while his colleagues celebrated and then dined with their British adversaries. It was a well earned party and he missed all of it.

When Arnold finally regained enough of his health, Washington appointed him, and inadvertently doomed him, as military commander of Philadelphia where he finally began to enjoy the good life. In his official capacity he was invited regularly to the social events of the City where he mingled with the gentry and was constantly exposed to their self-serving views. Heady stuff for a working class boy from New Haven.

Then the insidious rot began. As we discussed earlier, the upper class view was that all this uproar would eventually be resolved and they could resume their former pursuits, especially the pursuit of commerce. Although many had valuable contacts in England, they were not overt Loyalists (the overt Loyalists had fled with the British evacuation fleet). Rather, they were doing the smart thing, riding out the storm, perhaps speculating here and there on a settlement favorable to the Americans. Perhaps even investing in the potentially lucrative practice called privateering - piracy, legalized by letters from the United States government.

Some of the gentry also secretly maintained contacts with the British army.

Arnold was totally captivated. He joined their society, married into it - a much younger woman[18] - and began living well beyond his means. He sold administrative favors to support his lifestyle and was chastised by his critics in Congress.

He sold out completely for a promise of £20,000 and began a plan to betray and deliver the fort at West Point by asking for appointment as its commander.

Washington complied with the request; he liked the brash Arnold and appreciated more than most how much he had meant to the Revolution. He may have felt that political infighters like Gates had caused Arnold to receive less reward and more trouble than he deserved.

George knew first hand; Gates had tried to undercut him with Congress too.

Arnold's scheme proceeded smoothly as he began to reduce the West Point garrison strength. The scheme was uncovered at the last moment when conscientious sentries stopped and searched a young man who was found to be carrying the plans for the fort; plans drawn by Arnold personally. Washington happened to be visiting West Point at the time and, although sorely hurt by the betrayal, acted expeditiously to stop the plan. Arnold, aware that things were crashing down around him, fled to the British leaving his pregnant wife behind.

"Now the enigma - what convinced him to do it? Why did this great, proven patriot turn into a synonym for treason?"
"Why?"

"What do you think?"

"Maybe his wife talked him into it. She wasn't a patriot and her family members weren't either. Maybe her family talked to him too."

"You're surely partly right. She and her family were conduits to the British. In fact, she was very close to the young man who was captured carrying the plans."

"What happened to him? Did the Americans kill him?"

"Yes; his name was Major John Andre; he was hanged as a spy. When a soldier is captured behind enemy lines and not in uniform, he is automatically designated a spy and usually executed. However, sometimes spies are traded for captives from the other side. Andre was well connected and well liked and the British asked if we would trade for him. Washington said 'Yes, but only for one specific person'.

Can you guess who Washington named?"

"Someone captured at Ticonderoga?"

"Good guess, but no."
"I give up. Who?"

"Benedict Arnold."
"But he wasn't a captive."

"Correct, and Washington knew they wouldn't surrender him, even to save a popular young officer. I think George just wanted them to feel some of his pain. The British protested and accused the Americans of inhumanity, of course, but I don't think they were truly surprised or offended; after all, they had done the same thing to Nathan Hale and with less consideration.

But, back to 'why?' I think there are a number of possible reasons for Arnold's traitorous decision.

We know that Benedict Arnold had a difficult personality, that he was capable of great drive and achievement, that he had a large ego (somewhat justified), and that he aspired to a higher status in life. When he committed the same questionable actions as some others (like selling administrative favors), lesser men took the opportunity to nip at him and they probably would have brought him down if it weren't for George Washington's protection.
Like a hyena pack bringing down a lion.

It wasn't his style to curry their favor or to create his own pack. He clearly wasn't an adept politician.

So, what could be the reasons:
- Was his patriotism simply a cloak for his need for achievement and power, to be easily discarded when better opportunities came along?
Does patriotism often contain elements of self interest?
- Was his frustration at not being able to get his own way too much to accept; was he essentially a grown-up spoiled brat? Did he deceive himself into thinking that things would be different with the British?
- Was he eventually worn down and discouraged by his colleagues - their coolness, the personal attacks, the seemingly tolerated incompetence of some, the lack of dedication to the cause?
- Was this rejection compounded by the cordiality shown to him, feigned or real, by the gentry of Philadelphia? Except for Washington, they seemed to be the only ones who really accepted him. Was that because he looked up to them while he looked down on everyone else?
- Was he infatuated with his teenage wife whose outlook can be presumed to have been very pro-British?
- What was he willing to do for the money that he needed to maintain the lovely new way of life to which he had been introduced and which he likely felt obliged to continue to provide for his patrician wife?

- Did he undergo an epiphany, a revelation that the gentry's sense of reality was correct; that the war would end in a negotiated peace; that things would pretty much return to the way they were; and that those who had been smart and prudent would be the biggest winners and that those who gave the most, even their lives, would not be proportionally rewarded?"

"That's a long list of 'maybes'; which one is right?"
"Maybe a bit of all of them; it's not a simple problem."

"But you must have some idea; what do you think?"

"I think he went to Philadelphia hurting in body and spirit. He had always relied on his great endurance and spirit; he had sacrificed them for a cause that seemed to be stagnating, even turning in upon itself - a cause that was muddling along without him.

He may have based his earlier life upon the admonition that "hard work and self-denial" would be suitably rewarded. Since he had shown more of both characteristics than almost anyone else in the Revolution he had reason to expect recognition and position. When it failed to meet his expectations and was accompanied by criticism, now crippled and no longer young, he may have undergone a major change in outlook.

And now he had a lovely young wife, a glimpse at a better life that could be his, and a new vision on how to achieve that kind of life.

He had never done things tentatively. If he was going to abandon his past, he had one chance to make it pay - and to pay his considerable bills as well.

Others, like Daniel Morgan, became sick and disappointed and simply went home; or, like John Stark, was angry and went home. Benedict Arnold sold his reputation (some say his soul) and went over to the enemy.

His timing was even worse than his judgment. He abandoned the gloomy cause to which he had given so much just before it turned the corner into the light.

As a postscript, it has often been pointed out that Benedict Arnold was never accepted by the British military and was consigned to a lonely and bitter life. The reason given always has a moral: that traitors are viewed with repugnance and never really accepted anywhere.

I suspect that there are plenty of exceptions to that rule and that a simpler psychology is in effect here. Benedict Arnold couldn't form friendships and working relationships among the loosely structured Americans; I'm not surprised that he did even less well in aristocratic British society.

What do you think now?"

"I don't think he was a real patriot; I think he didn't think things through, he just did them. Maybe he just liked the action. Why was he always the one looking for challenges? Why was he the one to volunteer for the assignments that more 'sensible' men didn't want - Quebec, Stanwix, the charge at Saratoga?

Am I right Grampa?"

"I think you're on the right track. There is a theory that everyone is a combination of differing degrees of three driving elements - the need to achieve, the need for power, and the need for affiliation. There are no 'right' or 'better' combinations, but our different make-ups steer us in different directions. It's clear that Arnold had a huge need to achieve results, felt little need for affiliation (or suppressed what little he had), and probably wanted the sort of power that his ancestors had. I think he was driven by the achievement and power elements. The American cause gave him ample opportunity to achieve, but he became convinced by his wife's circle that the British Empire was the route to real power.

In the end, he revealed himself to be an opportunist, albeit an opportunist with great energy, stamina, and fearlessness.

It's another way of saying that I agree with you that patriotism was never his true driving force; that it was never real.

You might consider what combination of elements constitute a real patriot."

"What do you think, Grampa?"

"I'll leave that one to you."

Chapter 13
Interlude

The British world had been turned upside down and things rapidly deteriorated further. To their credit, the government faced the new challenges with the rationality and wisdom of experienced empire builders, but it was now time for damage control and the husbanding of their resources. In the three years that followed Saratoga:

- London issued orders that no more field battles were to be risked against the rebels. This was wiser than they knew as the American army had matured considerably, largely due to the efforts of the German drillmaster Baron von Steuben.
- Howe resigned and was replaced by Clinton, the last of the three generals that sailed over to bolster General Gage in Boston.
- A peace commission was sent from London to Philadelphia in June of 1778 supposedly empowered to offer the colonists every one of their demands short of full independence, including their own parliament and special status within the Empire.

It was too late, they had ignored their chance in 1775, and the Americans rejected them now without any consideration.

The American Congress was wise not to give the slightest show of interest to what must have been an intriguing offer. The British had demonstrated perfidy in past dealings and could have used prolonged negotiations to buy needed time, to diminish American momentum, and cast doubt upon the alliance in French minds.

The arrival of the Commission must have reinforced the certainty of the gentry that their vision of the future was correct; that reason was again beginning to prevail, and business might soon get back to normal.

- The British evacuated Philadelphia as part of a strategy to consolidate their forces as they entered a world war.
- Spain entered the war against Britain in 1779.
- Holland piled on in 1780.
- Hundreds of American privateers swarmed the waters around Britain preying on merchant shipping. John Glover and his men were among those who went to sea. The opportunity to make serious money was too tempting although, as usual, the risk was commensurate with the reward.

If captured by the British, their letters of legitimacy were from a government declared illegitimate itself and thus nearly worthless. The captured privateers probably wouldn't be hanged as pirates, but they would spend the rest of the war in foul, rotten, pestilent prison ships - if they could stay alive until the end of the war.

The land war in North America finally reached an equilibrium position after the pendulum of emotions had swung from undue American optimism to British overconfidence; in both cases with severe penalty.

The British were ensconced mainly in Quebec and in New York where they could be supplied by sea while Washington's army watched from the west and north. Clinton could not hope to engage and defeat the rebels in open combat and he was increasingly wary about the British claim that they could march with impunity anywhere they wished. Burgoyne had failed in his ambitious march and Cornwallis would run into difficulty later. Anyway, London had given him orders to stay put.

Washington was not much better off. He had no hope of successfully attacking the British positions, so he had to sit, wait, and continue to train his men.

For the present, the war had reached a stalemate; the armies mostly sat or sniped at each other while the European navies fought around the globe and the financial managers worried about their depleted treasuries. A war of attrition was underway between two opponents both approaching financial crisis.

On the brighter side, the worst days were past for the Americans. The army had been transformed from unreliable, short term militia men into mostly trained "Continentals"; and morale had improved.

Chapter 14
The War Moves South

The first British priority in 1778 was the Caribbean. Reputedly, the revenue from Jamaica was worth more to Britain in that year than the combined revenue from all 13 North American colonies would have been. The French fleet was active and no colony was safe. Troops were needed that could respond quickly to challenges and New York was too far away to provide them.

The long sea voyage from New York was doubly damning - it took nearly as long to alert General Clinton of a need as it would take for him to send troops in response. Accordingly, the Colonial Office in London ordered him to send troops southward and nearly half his army was split between St Lucia and the attack on Savannah, Georgia. The latter would be used as a staging area for the Caribbean as well as for its original *raison d'etre*, an impediment to the Spanish in Florida.

Meanwhile, in the British Parliament, opposition to the war was growing more strident. From the beginning, the dominant Tory party had favored strong, punitive measures in dealing with the unrest in the Colonies while the minority Whigs urged negotiation and compromise. This open difference of opinion undoubtedly led many on both sides of the ocean to see accommodation as the likely eventual outcome, once the Americans showed that they could not be defeated militarily.

The Colonial Minister, Lord Germain, now needed a rationale for a continuing confrontation with the Americans; he could no longer simply ignore the challenges thrown by the Whigs. The position that he developed appealed to both emotion and a line of logic.

The emotional appeal was for the loyalty Britain owed to her many subjects in North America (the Loyalists) who had opposed the Revolution, had openly supported the British position, and had risked all for their loyalty. For Britain to end hostilities and acknowledge American independence would be to abandon them to an unpleasant fate - at the least, humiliation and the loss of property; in some instances, death.

The line of logic then extended to a policy that stated that since they were not to be abandoned, and since Britain was strained both financially and militarily, the Loyalists must rise up and participate to a much greater degree in the conflict. Because there was assumed to be a Loyalist majority in the southern colonies, that was where the new policy would be initiated. It was, not coincidentally, where Britain had to go anyway in order to protect her Caribbean colonies.

There were many influential Loyalist voices assuring their Tory friends of the dedication and nascent strength of those left behind - if only the British army would support them. It was a deceptive exaggeration, but one that the Tories found useful, so it wasn't questioned with sufficient diligence.

Another motive is conceivable. Britain, recognizing that it was now possible that the northern colonies might be lost, could have hoped to salvage the southern colonies for the Empire. The British also tried, unsuccessfully, to stake a claim to the western lands by building and occupying small forts there.

Germain's position was successfully sold in Britain and the Whig opposition was quieted for the while. British sensitivities about loyalty could be assuaged while the war, with still the hope of eventual success, could be carried at a reduced cost by the Loyalists. The logic was somewhat circular and based upon seriously flawed assumptions, but it prevailed for the moment and averted a governmental crisis.

The assumption of a significant Loyalist uprising was based upon the British army having been able to march easily through the South and because there were known concentrations of Loyalists in the upland Carolinas.

Actually, the South had been more indifferent to the Revolution than loyal to the Crown and there were as many pockets of anti-British sentiment as there were Loyalists. But, for a while, things went very well for the British, seemingly proving the validity of Germain's position.

Many of the settlers in the Carolinas were of Scottish descent, either directly or via the plantations in Ireland. The Irish branch of the Church of England had influenced legislation outrageously, by current standards, on behalf of their favorites. Although hardest on Catholics, other Protestant sects, Presbyterians and Methodists in particular, probably lost more since the Catholics by this time had already lost nearly everything and had little else to lose. This injustice was the impetus for this first wave of Irish immigrants to America. Mostly Protestants, they had an "Irish" identity and only later changed it to "Scots-Irish" to differentiate themselves from the later waves of Catholic Irish.

John Kennedy is usually thought of as the first U S President of Irish ancestry, but he was preceded by at least 8 others including Jackson, Polk, and Wilson[19] .

The first immigrants to the Carolinas naturally built near the coast and many developed successful plantations. They opposed the thought of increased British oversight of their lives; they also had little affinity for the newer arrivals who carved small farms from the higher land to the west. The newer settlers, proving the adage that "my enemy's enemy is my friend", were typically pro-British.

The frontiersmen even further west were anti British. Firstly, because of London's interference with their expansion into "Indian" lands and later because of the British instigation of the Cherokee nation whose warriors raided homes and small settlements along the western borders from Georgia to Virginia with a savage fury that became legend.

Despite their differences, there was considerable social stability among the settler groups because the issues weren't serious enough to fight over and a feud, once started, could cause everyone to lose. In fact, Loyalists and rebel frontiersmen sometimes joined forces to defend their homes and families from the greater threat of the marauding Cherokees who raided and scalped with little regard for the political inclinations of their victims.

The British injected themselves into this societal stew and called upon the Loyalists to rise up in support. As has so often happened, the injection of a new element unbalanced the social order, polarized the factions, and started something very similar to the clan warfare of their ancestors. The stubborn Celtic spirit displayed itself in fierce battles, selfless devotion to both causes, and atrocities reminiscent of the darkest episodes in Scottish history.

Charleston

In 1776, the first British attempt to capture Fort Moultrie in the harbor, and thence Charleston, South Carolina failed. General Clinton, directing the attack, eventually abandoned the effort and sailed back to New York.

A key element of the plan was to demolish the fort by naval bombardment. The simple fort had been constructed of the only materials readily available, the soft spongy logs from the Palmetto trees. Serendipitously, these logs proved to be ideal as the cannon balls rebounded off them, leaving small dents, and doing none of the damage that they would have inflicted on stone or harder wood. For everyone but the British, it must have been hilarious to watch. And to add to the British frustration, three of the bombarding ships were lost in the battle.

"Now you know why the Palmetto tree is on the state flag of South Carolina."

A second attempt in 1779 by a small British force was quickly abandoned when the Americans appeared in superior numbers.

In early 1780 Clinton again appeared off Charleston, this time with an overwhelming force of men and ships. Carefully, he surrounded the American force under General Benjamin Lincoln stationed within the City. Fort Moultrie fell to siege by land based forces and when Bannistre Tarleton's Loyalists defeated the rebel garrison to the north of the city, the plug was in the bottle. Lincoln was in the same position as Gage four years previously in Boston - except for one huge difference - he didn't have a navy to take him away to safety.

Rather than subject the City and its supportive citizenry to destruction from bombardment, Lincoln surrendered the entire American army of over 5,000, a defeat nearly as great as Burgoyne's at Saratoga, but without as serious a political fallout.

A more capable leader than Lincoln might have found a way to extricate his troops and escape surrender.

Camden and Gates - More Bad News

Reacting to the disaster at Charleston, Congress appointed General Gates, whose reputation as the victor at Saratoga exceeded his contributions and capabilities, as leader of the Southern Army. Gates was not liked or respected by Washington and other officers, in part because he had tried to discredit Washington in order to supplant him. Although Washington was overall army commander, Congress neither discussed their choice nor told him of the appointment; a poor performance by a group that had risen to heights on other occasions.

Gates assumed command on July 25, 1780 and, with insufficient knowledge of the situation, started immediately towards the British outpost in Camden, South Carolina. Maybe he had been influenced by his own press clippings and had decided that defeating the British was easier than he had previously believed. He was out to shed the "Granny" label and enhance his already bright image. He marched his men through barren country despite being low on rations and ran into a larger British army than he expected, under the direct command of General Cornwallis. The British had left Camden to meet him on the open field.

Gates still outnumbered Cornwallis by nearly 2 to 1 on paper, but the larger part of his army consisted of unreliable militia from Virginia and North Carolina. Daniel Morgan would have intermixed his militia and regulars, but Gates didn't. When the British attacked, the militia on the American left ran and the Continentals were then slaughtered. At the first sign of trouble, Gates turned his horse north and rode as though the devil was after him.

Horatio Gates had managed to destroy what was left of the American Southern Army and his own reputation in just about three weeks.

A Ray of Hope - King's Mountain

Lord Germain's plan was working beautifully, so Cornwallis had no option but to attempt to parlay his success, although he probably knew that the circumstances that created that success might not be able to be duplicated. With momentum on his side and the rebel army dissolved, he began a campaign to add North Carolina to the growing Loyalist region which now claimed South Carolina and Georgia.

But there were still those pesky irregulars who raided at will in guerrilla style and discredited the claim that the region was safely Loyalist. Some operated in the swamp lands near the coast and had almost romantic images and titles like "The Swamp Fox", Francis Marion.
Sir Walter Scott would have loved to have written about them.
Others were the frontiersmen in the west who had begun coordinating their operations with very positive results.

As he marched into North Carolina unopposed, Cornwallis sent a detachment of Loyalists under Major Patrick Ferguson westward to intimidate the frontiersmen. Ferguson sent word to the mountaineers to stop all their operations immediately or he would march into the mountains and destroy them and their settlements.

They were not impressed and decided to save him the trouble by coming to him (and also keeping the battle off their own turf). Ferguson retreated eastward towards Cornwallis until he reached a fort-like plateau at King's Mountain, just over the state line in South Carolina.

For the British, it was Bennington all over again, only worse.

Both sides had about 1,000 men. The mountaineers decided to operate as individual units under their various leaders (most bearing the self-appointed title of Colonel) and crept through the forest until the mountain was completely surrounded by guerrilla bands. The strategy, besides feeling comfortable, suggested that they did not want to drive the Loyalists back to Cornwallis; they wanted to annihilate them.

The battle was pure frontier with marksmen picking off the British from all sides; firing from protective cover. When the British reacted by charging down a section of the mountain in overwhelming force the frontiersmen simply melted into the forest, daring their enemies to follow them into that fatal trap. The sniping then resumed, following the retreating Loyalists back to camp. "Colonel" William Campbell's mountaineers saw some of the heaviest action.

Ferguson was magnificent in action, but eventually he fell riddled with bullets and the Loyalists decided they had had enough.

But now came the worst news of all - surrender was not an option!

This was clan warfare against an enemy that subscribed to "Tarleton's quarter". These enemy soldiers were not regulars from London or Germany who were there, possibly not even by choice, to do a job. These were Loyalist enemies who had reveled in the bloody job that they had been doing against both soldier and civilian; against man, woman, and child.

It was pay back time and the mountaineers proceeded to execute the prisoners until their leaders gave the order to stop.

About 600 Loyalists survived the battle and the aftermath. The ambulatory were marched off and the others left to most likely die. In the days that followed, those prisoners who were specifically identified for past viciousness were also executed. Ferguson and his detachment ceased to exist.

The frontiersmen returned to their mountains.

Patrick Ferguson was a very capable officer who had, among other things, invented an accurate, rapid firing, breech loading musket for which the British army saw no use. Ironically, if his men had been armed with his musket, they might have survived.

Reintroducing Nathaniel Greene

Having tried and failed as military strategists, Congress now asked Washington to decide who should replace Gates. There must have been a tormenting temptation to gloat, but George did as he always did and went forward doing his best for the country. He did very well; he nominated the man who was perhaps second only to himself in capability, Nathaniel Greene of Rhode Island.

Greene had served the cause valiantly from the beginning. Sickness alone had kept him out of action at Brooklyn and he had served many effective years since as Quartermaster, probably the most frustrating job in the Army as he tried to scrounge enough from the various colonies to keep the ragged army alive.

All armies must provide for the soldier's stomachs and in revolutionary times it was a doubly difficult task. Not only did the supplies have to be coaxed from a populace that could only be paid in worthless paper money, but then the supplies had to be transported through a countryside with little infrastructure and armed opposition.

Greene had learned how to handle the supply problems and his close association with Washington allowed him to absorb his commander's tactics and philosophy. Both would serve him and his country well in the months ahead.

The appointment of Nathaniel Greene as commander of the Southern Army marks the beginning of the end for the British in the American colonies.

Daniel Morgan Again! - Cowpens

Cornwallis was an intelligent military leader who prosecuted Germain's plan well, but probably knew that it was limited in applicability, if not flawed outright in the long run. Accordingly, he correctly interpreted the message from King's Mountain and retreated back into South Carolina.

The "army" that Greene found was in tatters. However, he had some good, reliable officers including Kosciuszko, William Washington (George's cousin), and Daniel Morgan.

Despite considerable pain from the effects of his hard life, Morgan had returned from a furlough to support Gates, whom he personally liked. Morgan, like others during the war, was disappointed in not receiving the promotion to brigadier general that he felt he deserved after Saratoga and

resigned. No one in Congress opposed his promotion, but rules had been established tying the number of brigadiers from each state to its contribution of soldiers.
There were no slots left for Virginians, including Morgan, so they asked him to take a furlough until something could be worked out. It was a welcome suggestion as he had become so lame from sciatica and other assorted aches and wounds that he was nearly immobile.
 Now he was back - just in time.

Greene sent Morgan's command, including William Washington's cavalry, westward and Cornwallis sent "Bloody" Tarleton's infamous Loyalist Greens after him. Morgan turned to confront Tarleton with a river at his back. It would seem to be an unwise battleground, leaving no avenue for retreat. Some feel that he didn't want to risk being attacked while crossing the river.

 "But you think otherwise?"
 "I wonder if he felt that his troops could defeat the British if the militia didn't run so he placed them where they couldn't run."

Unlike Gates, Morgan was an experienced militia leader and he deployed his men skillfully and then insured that everyone knew his plan.
 The plan called for the front line to consist of riflemen who had an unimpeded view and could pick off the British and Loyalist officers from a distance. As the British advanced, the sharpshooters would withdraw leaving a line of South Carolina militia of whom Morgan asked only one thing - to hold their ground long enough to fire three volleys and then they also could retreat. By giving them a distinct assignment, he expected that they would not panic and flee before they did some damage to the oncoming enemy.

But he had a more devious intent; he wanted the militia to be seen leaving the field. In past battles that had been the signal for the British to charge, turning the battle into a rout.

Morgan personally visited his men around their campfires the night before the battle, chatting, encouraging, explaining his battle plan; some say he didn't sleep all night.

The plan worked beautifully. The riflemen performed as they always did with punishing accuracy. The militia fired three volleys and then seemed to wilt before the British. For the British it was *deja vu* - beating these farm boys was easy - they charged.

The charge was met head-on by the counter charge of William Washington's cavalry from behind the hill that hid them and the British charge was crushed. The British infantry pressed on the center and were surprised by the steady opposition of the Continentals placed there by Morgan.

Now things began to happen fast. The British left flank pushed back the Virginia militia and charged in for the kill; but the Virginians reformed behind a hill and dropped them with volleys reminiscent of Bunker Hill. Next, the South Carolina militia, having withdrawn after their three volleys, reformed and threw their weight behind their Virginia brethren as the cavalry raced over from the other side of the field.

That did it! The British and Loyalists broke and ran and mopping up was all that remained to be done.

Cowpens wasn't a large battle, with only about 1,000 on each side. But it produced three important results:
- It destroyed the infamous Tarleton Greens, the scourge of the Carolinas and Cornwallis' eyes and ears in the countryside. Nearly all the British and Loyalists were killed

or captured. Although Tarleton escaped and the Greens' losses were replaced with new men, their reputation for invincibility was shattered.
- It ended the dream of a Loyalist uprising to bear the burden of the war. Those Loyalists who didn't get the message after King's Mountain clearly had it now.
- It shredded Lord Germain's plan and, more importantly, the argument that kept the Whig opposition in Parliament at bay. One more episode of bad news could bring down the government and end the war.

"Is that why you've built your story around some of these smaller battles?"

"Exactly! I've concentrated on those events, mostly battles, that were pivotal - Bunker Hill, Brooklyn, Sarasota, of course, and now the South. If any of them had gone differently it would have changed the course of world history and the dream of democracy.

More intriguingly, some of these battles pivoted upon even smaller events within them - Stark's men behind the rail fence at Bunker Hill, for instance.

Have you heard the saying "For want of a nail the shoe was lost ...?"

"Yep, and I see what you mean; I think it's called chaos theory in math."

Back to Square One

Greene continued to employ his commander's strategy of inflicting wounds upon his enemy without risking the battle that could destroy his army. Battles were fought, sometimes in cooperation with Marion's and the other guerrilla bands, but none was decisive.

By the summer of 1781, the Loyalists were gone and many of the British and Germans, decimated by bullets and tropical diseases, and bereft of food, were back to the seacoast cities of Charleston and Savannah where they could be supplied by the navy. They had gained nothing of permanence and Germain's vision of a Loyalist counter revolution had proven to be a mirage.

Cornwallis and his small army was in Virginia where he somehow concluded that he might fare better. He had previously recommended it as a target to Clinton; Clinton later claimed that he had opposed it as too risky.

Going there now was not a good idea.

Chapter 15
Gotcha!

1779 and 1780 passed and now it was 1781. Washington had managed the war as best he could; as well as anyone could. Far too weak to attack the main British position in New York, he camped on their western flank where he could challenge any landward moves and from where he could send reinforcements to other theaters as the needs and opportunities arose. He had too little support from the individual states and too few men in his army to do more.

In May 1781, Washington was notified by the French admiral, deGrasse, that his fleet would be out of the Caribbean and available to the Americans for a few weeks that fall; perhaps deGrasse felt that there were better places than the Caribbean to spend the hurricane season. For once, Washington would briefly have naval support, perhaps even control of the sea. How best to exploit this opportunity?

Previously, the French had landed an army of about 4,000 men in America, led by the Count de Rochambeau. Rochambeau had set up camp in Newport, Rhode Island

and waited for the right opportunity to use his army meaningfully. He did not want them shot up in a war of attrition; that was for the Americans with their seemingly endless supply of militia men who would show up for battle and then disappear.

The British fleet denied him movement by sea.

Washington had hoped to someday challenge the British in New York and he asked Rochambeau to consider joining him. Rochambeau marched his men to the New York area where they waited while the leaders studied the possibilities.

Meanwhile, Cornwallis, having encountered little resistance in Virginia, was becoming enthusiastic about the chances of capturing this important Colony. He asked for reinforcements from New York and received over 4,000 men giving him a total of about 7,000. One of the officers sent was the new British brigadier general, Benedict Arnold.

Apparently the concept of winning over the local populace died at Cowpens and good old fashioned British butt kicking rule-by-intimidation was again the strategy. Arnold led a raiding party to Richmond, torched it, and returned to the British seacoast command center at Portsmouth, Virginia. His assignment in the army seemed to be hit and run raids on small towns and cities, including New London in his native Connecticut.

If he had any apologists at the time of his treason, his raiding must have quieted them all.

Washington responded to the threat to his home state by sending a force of about 1,000 men under the command of his friend and protégé, the young French aristocrat, the Marquis de Lafayette. The choice of Lafayette may also have been a gesture of solidarity to Rochambeau and a further reason for the French to support this campaign.

Once on the scene, Lafayette began to attract militia men, including "Colonel" William Johnson (of King's Mountain fame) with more than 500 frontier riflemen. Washington sent General "Mad" Anthony Wayne's Pennsylvania Continentals next, bringing Lafayette's total to about 5,000 - not all dependable, but a significant force - a force large enough to keep the British at bay.

Suddenly the plan came together for Washington!
- An attack on New York was not feasible; it was too strongly defended. The other large British army was in Virginia; could that be the target? Rochambeau wrote to de Grasse.
- de Grasse informed Washington that he would sail to Chesapeake Bay in mid August and leave in mid October.
- LaFayette appeared to be able to keep Cornwallis pinned down on the coast for the meantime.

Washington sprang into action, his enthusiasm restored. An opportunity to relieve years of frustration and defeat was at hand. His basic plan had two needs:
1. Deceive Clinton into thinking that New York was the target of the American-French initiative so he would neither reinforce Cornwallis nor strike forth with his army.
2. Assemble enough land and sea forces against Cornwallis in Virginia to insure a decisive victory. That meant:
    - A long overland march for the American and French armies.
    - French siege cannons shipped from Newport, Rhode Island to Virginia.
    - The arrival of the French fleet to drive off any attempt by the British fleet to provide support or escape.

All elements of the plan worked perfectly. Extensive arrangements were made to build a permanent French camp in New Jersey. It was a masterful performance that captivated British attention. The march south was two weeks along before Clinton could be convinced that it was not a feint. The first army elements reached LaFayette on September 14th. Cornwallis could not escape by land.

Meanwhile, the British fleet, also in the Caribbean, realized that the French had left and thought it highly likely that they were up to something that was not in Britain's best interests. The British sailed north, perhaps with the dual goals of checking on the French and avoiding hurricanes as well. Without realizing it, they passed the French fleet. Therefore, when they checked into Chesapeake Bay it was empty so they quickly went on, certain that New York was the target. It wasn't, and by the time they returned to the Chesapeake on September 5th, the French were at anchor. A short naval battle ensued, costing the British one ship before they withdrew from the superior French force.

Washington had control of the sea!

While the fleets were fighting, the shipment of siege cannon was delivered without incident. DeGrasse unloaded another 2,500 French soldiers giving LaFayette an army now larger than Cornwallis'; and more ships were added to the French fleet.

The American/French army moved close on September 28th and the siege cannons opened up a week later. Less than two weeks of incessant pounding from textbook siege maneuvers forced the British surrender.

After six mostly painful years Washington had his day!

The actual surrender was a classic in protocol; humorous, if it weren't for the other emotions that ruled the occasion.

Cornwallis felt unwell (understandably) and sent General O'Hara to do the surrendering for him, probably with instructions to surrender to the noble French general, not the rebel riffraff.

O'Hara rode to Rochambeau and began his surrender speech. Rochambeau, seemingly embarrassed by the lack of either knowledge or courtesy by the British, directed him to the army commander, George Washington.

When O'Hara began to surrender again, Washington sent him to General Benjamin Lincoln. If Cornwallis was going to send a staff officer, then he could surrender to a staff officer. He did, and the proceedings were finally complete.

Lincoln was chosen deliberately; he was the general who had been forced to surrender the American Southern Army at Charleston.

Chapter 16
How it Finally Ended.

If asked, most people would answer that the surrender of the British army at Yorktown, Virginia ended the Revolution and established the United States of America as a separate and independent nation.

It was true, that it took a significant force out of the picture but the British Army still sat in an impregnable position in New York and could provide, if reinforced, the springboard for continued action. Another British army was stationed in Canada.

The King was prepared to fight for as long as it took.

But Britain was not an absolute monarchy any longer and the British Parliament had finally had enough. The government fell and Lord Germain was out as Colonial Minister. No more money would be spent fighting the rebellion. No military action would proceed. Peace negotiations would begin. That was 1781.

The Stamp Act had been passed in 1765 with the hope of eventually raising revenue of 60,000 pounds. The Revolution that followed had cost 100 million pounds and had been a terrible mistake as well as a terrible investment. It was time to stop the bleeding, both literally and figuratively, and get back to the business of running an empire.

The British Empire was run well and was capable of making hard decisions. The decision to end the military losses in the American colonies was made and it was left to the negotiators to make the best of the situation.

Washington, aware of British tactics, moved his army to Newburgh, New York as a counterbalance to Clinton. The Americans would negotiate from the strength of an intact army, not from weakness.

Nearly two years of negotiations, conducted more like a chess game than a business transaction, ensued. Hostilities had essentially ceased and the British politicians were in no hurry to conclude anything today if they thought that tomorrow might bring more favorable conditions. Besides, they wanted to explore the possibilities of squeezing the Americans by concluding separate treaties with their allies.

It's also very possible that they hoped that the coalition of States would quickly crumble and that their army could easily step into the vacuum.

Throughout all the laborious debate, the British asked nothing for their Iroquois allies. Perhaps they were still angry about the unreliability of the natives, it's far more likely that they were indifferent to the fate of native peoples who were no longer of any use to them. When you're running an empire you have to make business decisions and loyalty is hard to justify financially.

Worse, if possible, was the continuing deceit practiced upon the Iroquois. Needing their support, the British dealt with them as with a sovereign nation, plying them with gifts and alcohol, and never telling them that their lands were already considered to be part of British North America. It came as a considerable shock to the natives to find that their Great Father had transferred their lands to the Americans in the peace treaty.

The Confederacy of the Six Iroquois Nations was dead.

It wasn't until September 3, 1783 that the peace treaty was formally signed in Paris, more than eight years after the battle on Lexington Green, seven years after the colonists had the audacity to declare independence, and two years after the British surrender at Yorktown.

What to do now? The Revolution was fought in reaction to British domination - direct control by an unrepresentative Parliament as well as an insidiously growing Britishness among the wealthy gentry (whose wealth was tied to British trade) and the growing influence of the Church of England in North America.

Evidence of this Church influence can be seen in the attempt to replace the popular but too independently inclined Puritan missionaries to the Iroquois with more reliable Anglican priests[20].

For decades after independence, the Episcopal Church (successor to the Church of England) continued to provide very many of the capable and influential leaders of the new Republic.

The Revolution had been won but a vision and plan for the future was needed.

Following the peace treaty, the United States was a fragile infant[21] having just survived a difficult birth. All the divisive issues that had been suppressed by either wartime necessity or British mandate now began to surface and confront the politicians in the Continental Congress.

The smaller minds focused on the local issues, the special interests of their friends and supporters, and their own opportunities. Fortunately, statesmen with a broader view were also present, but a bickering stagnation set in that threatened to tear apart the weak bonds of mutual self-interest had been holding them together.

Among the pressing issues were:
- Government organization. The Continental Congress didn't have the power, authority, or structure to manage a country. But there was a problem - no model existed for the democracy that the leaders of the time idealized, each somewhat differently, in their individual minds. Very little like it had existed since the tiny Athenian city-state in ancient times and even that was an aristocratic republic that doubted the wisdom of true democracy.

The Icelandic Althing was democratic but insufficiently structured for use on the scale of the United States and probably little known at that time.

Ironically, the best available model existed in North America - the organization of the six Iroquois nations; an organization that had functioned successfully until the conflicting stresses of the American Revolution tore it apart.

So, the Americans had a huge new land in a greedy, contentious world; a rather vague idea of how they wanted to govern it; and a nearly blank sheet of paper to design upon.[22]

On the positive side, they had external pressures that encouraged unity for their common good; a rich, open land that allowed generosity in negotiation; and a sufficiency of principled leaders.

- Very different economies and cultures among the States. Although these issues were temporarily papered over, the differences festered until they were violently confronted. The paramount issue of slavery nearly destroyed the country through civil war less than a century later.[23]
- The western lands. This problem was a stew of rich, beckoning lands, militant native populations, British colonial charters of overlapping and questionable validity (some granting strips of land all the way to the Pacific Ocean), and foreign claims.
- Financing the government.

Eventually, one of the greatest documents in world history was created - the Constitution of the United States. It was written so thoughtfully that it has guided this country through 200 years of challenges and events that were unforeseeable to its creators. It became a model for many other countries as the seeds of democracy were blown forth.

The "framers" of our Constitution succeeded so well because they understood unchanging human nature. Founded upon respect for the worth and rights of the individual, it addressed the timeless threats to that freedom, among them:
- Government sanctioned religious domination.
- Government tyranny and oppression.

"The Constitution has kept us free all these years?"

"The Constitution is a blueprint for government, a very well drawn blueprint to be sure, but it's still only lines on paper. The American people, devoted to the principles in the Constitution, are the ones who have kept us free.

It is the duty of every generation of Americans to remain vigilant. The seductive appeal of solving current problems by abridging personal freedom is as present today as it was in 1780. It is most virulent in small matters and when used against small groups; matters to which the larger population is indifferent.

We are a large, complex society and need many laws to regulate the interaction of people, businesses, and government. We have, however, jealously resisted regulation of our private lives and choices; even to preserving the right to do things that are dangerous or unwise.

These rights are rare in world history and precious; once yielded, they may be lost forever."

Washington's Greatness

It has been said that all revolutions have eventually turned upon themselves - except the American Revolution. "All" is probably not correct, but one can think of many examples of military success followed by political dissension leading to anarchy, civil war, and dictatorship. Perhaps some in the British government were betting on this when they ceased fighting.

One can imagine "Let the Americans muddle about for a bit. They'll eventually self-destruct and return to sensible British rule."

King George envisioned a different outcome. There would be turmoil in government (he was right) and George Washington would remedy things by establishing himself as king.

Why not? At that time monarchies were just about the only functional government model around.

George III also said that if Washington resisted seizing the opportunity that was sure to arise then he was the "greatest man in the world".

"That would never happen in America."

"Never say never.
You're right that it didn't happen, but it seemed to come perilously close."

"When was this?"

"In the dark days following the end of hostilities. Government operations sputtered along poorly with a despair that matched the poverty of the people holding their nearly worthless paper money. Men of capability, action, and vision were impatient, especially those who were officers in the army. They proposed that George Washington, with the army's support, seize control and straighten out the mess.
It has happened a lot in more recent times; it's called a military dictatorship."

"Wow. But it didn't happen. Why didn't it happen?"

"Because of one man - George Washington. Remember when I said that the Continental Congress couldn't have realized how great a choice they had made when they appointed him commander of the army? Remember what King George said about greatness?

Washington declared his loyalty to the government, the people, and the cause to which he had given so much and for which he had risked everything. He rejected his officers' proposal and rebuked them for suggesting it.

It's possible that Washington felt that the principles that the people had fought for would not be abandoned for anyone, including himself. Perhaps he felt that if he seized power a civil war would follow, undoing all the gains of the Revolution. But there is no evidence that this was his concern - probably because he never allowed his thought process to get that far.

No, it appears that he was motivated only by the principle of democracy for which he fought. Perhaps because he was already rich he felt less need for personal gain; perhaps he had reached an age when serenity had a stronger appeal than ambition.

But I think King George had it right - George Washington was the greatest man in the world."

His moral path led to a legacy of adulation and lasting fame that he never could have achieved by forcing even the most benign dictatorship upon the people.

In keeping with the concept of the victor's spoils, the new American government told the natives of the five Iroquois nations that supported the British that the peace treaty gave them no rights and that they should assume that they had lost everything, including their lands, and that they should see what they could negotiate. I suppose it could have been worse; if it had been England or Ireland in Cromwell's time, the losers would likely have lost their lives as well.

Faced with few options, the natives traded much of their land for transient goods and drifted away. Some tribes went to Canada.

The one Indian nation that supported the Americans, the Oneidas, was granted its lands in central New York in perpetuity by a grateful nation. Further, it was legislated that those lands could not be sold or taken for any purpose without Federal approval.

Well, perpetuity isn't as long as it used to be and over the following two centuries the reserved land shrunk from around 250,000 acres to less than 100.

And that brings our story to the present. The remaining Oneidas have brought the question of ownership before the

Supreme Court of the United States and have received a judgment that all the land transfers were illegal. None had the required Federal approval!

The last battle of the Revolution, over ownership of a large part of central New York State, is now underway.

"I hate to admit it Grampa, but that is a great story. Where did you learn all that stuff?"

"I'll resist quoting platitudes about age. I was lucky and had parents and teachers who were interested in history.

Also, early on, I formed the vision that the story that I just told you completely encompassed the Revolution. Since then, everything that I have read has fit neatly into place."

"There's only one thing wrong."
"What?"

"I still have a test to pass."
"And, for once, I won't ask 'why?'"

Appendix 1
Table of Dates

I. War in New England
1775 - April 19 British march to Lexington and Concord.
- May 10 Capture of Fort Ticonderoga.
- June 17 Battle of Bunker Hill.
- August American invasion of Canada begins.

1776 - March 17 British evacuate Boston

II. War in New York
1776 - August British capture New York City.
- December 25 Americans defeat British at Trenton.

1777 - June Burgoyne begins march to Albany.
- July 5 Americans abandon Ticonderoga.
- August 16 Americans defeat Germans at Bennington.
- August British advance in west stopped at Fort Stanwix.
- October 7 Second British defeat at Saratoga; Burgoyne surrenders.

III. Interlude
1778 - February 6 France formally recognizes the United States.

- December 29 British capture Savannah.

1779

IV. War in the South
1780 - May 12 British capture Charleston and American army.

- August 16 Americans defeated at Camden, South Carolina.

- October 7 American frontiersmen win at King's Mountain, S. C.

- December 2 Greene takes command of the southern army.

1781 - January 17 Americans defeat British and Loyalists at Cowpens.

- May The French fleet offers help in autumn.

- October 17 British surrender to Americans and French at Yorktown.

V. Peace Negotiations
1783 - September 3 Peace treaty signed in Paris.

Appendix 2
The Cast of Characters[24]

This appendix is provided for those who would like to know more about the many heroes and occasional villain in this story.

Some went on to great achievement and fame; some built fortunes and others failed in the attempt; some returned to a simple lifestyle; some died soon after the War and many lived to an age remarkable for the time; and some I have not yet been able to find anywhere.

I. Early Settlers

Baltimore, George Calvert, 1st Baron. Born c1580 in Kipling, Yorkshire, England.
  1597. Graduated from Trinity College, Oxford.
  1606. Began public career as a linguist/private secretary.
  1617. Knighted by James I.
  1621. After much involvement in North American colonization, he founded a small colony in Newfoundland which failed partially because of the extreme climate.

1625. Converted to Catholicism. He resigned from public office in an atmosphere of increasing Puritan pressure. A large landowner in England and Ireland, he was given an Irish barony by King James.

1629. Given land adjoining Virginia by Charles I which he named Maryland in honor of Charles' wife Henrietta Maria. Although he wished to provide sanctuary for persecuted Catholics, the Charter he created mentioned no faith specifically and espoused toleration for all faiths. It also gave supreme power to the founders of the Colony, not the Crown.

He died 4-15-1632 in London at age 52. After his death:

1649. The Maryland Assembly passed the Toleration Act guaranteeing religious liberty to all who "accepted the doctrine of the Trinity".

1689. A Protestant rebellion, led by John Coode, overthrew the Colonial government following allegations of Catholic favoritism.

1691. The Crown rescinded the authority to govern Maryland that it had given to the Lords of Baltimore.

Oglethorpe, James Edward. Born 12-22-1696 in London.

He attended school at Eton and Oxford.

1714. Joined the Austrian Army and fought against Turkey.

1722. Became a member of Parliament.

1729. Appointed to investigate conditions in debtors' prisons.

1732. Received (with others) a charter to found the colony of Georgia. Although its chief purpose was to provide a buffer for Britain against the Spanish in Florida, he also intended it as a new start for insolvent debtors and a haven for others, primarily oppressed European Protestants.

1740 & 1743. Attacked but failed to capture St Augustine, Florida.

1742. Defeated Spanish invaders at Bloody Marsh.

1743. Returned to England and was promoted to Major General.

1745. Failed in a campaign against Jacobites and retired from military.

1754. retired from Parliament.

He died on 7-1-1785 in Essex, England at age 89.

Penn, William. Born 10-24-1644 in Ruscombe, Berkshire, England.

He was the son of a British admiral and spent his youth in Macroom, Ireland on an estate given to his father by Oliver Cromwell.

1657. His first exposure to Quaker doctrine.

1660. Entered Oxford but was expelled for religious nonconformity. He toured Europe and spent 18 months at the French Protestant University of Saumur in Anjou. Upon return to England, he studied law for a year.

1667. Sent to manage family estates in Ireland. He joined the Quakers and was imprisoned.

1669. Imprisoned in the Tower of London for his anti-Trinity writings. While in prison he wrote his greatest book "No Cross, No Crown". He was released the same year.

1670. In a climate of persecution of all religious sects by the Church of England he was again arrested but so ably argued his position that the jury freed him only to be, itself, fined and imprisoned. The case then expanded into a test of the rights of Englishmen and the independence of the jury system. Upon appeal, the Lord Chief Justice found for Penn and the jury.

- Inherits all Penn estates upon the death of his brother.

1672. Married Gulielma Springett, a daughter of a famous Quaker family. He continued as an estate owner and fervent Quaker writer and preacher.

1675-81. Oversees properties in New Jersey.

1681. Granted Pennsylvania by King Charles II in return for cancellation of debts owed by the Crown to his father's estate. He saw America as a fresh start for the principles that were not tolerated in England.

- He wrote a colonial charter that included representative government, tolerance for all who believed in God, eligibility for public office for all who believed in Jesus Christ, free elections, trial by jury, and a humane penal code.

- He held friendly meetings with the native people.

1684. Returned to England for a boundary dispute with Lord Baltimore.

1692-94. Pennsylvania put under New York control as Penn was under suspicion of being a Jacobite.

1693. Proposed an organization of European nations (including Russia and Turkey) for the peaceful settlement of disputes.

1694. A widower, he married Hannah Callowhill.

1696. Conceived of a plan for the union of the American colonies, anticipating the American Constitution by nearly a century.

1699. Returned to address/settle chronic problems including:

• Lower counties (now Delaware) chafed under Quaker rule. He gave them virtual independence.

• English anger against the Quakers for refusing to participate in military operations.

1701. A new charter is forced upon Pennsylvania. Penn returned to England leaving his secretary, James Logan, in charge.

1707-08. Sent to debtors prison after an employee embezzled his money.

1712. Incapacitated by a stroke.

He died on 8-10-1718 in Roscombe, Berkshire, England at age 73.

II. American, French, and Allied Forces

Allen, Ethan. Born 1-10-1738 in Litchfield, Connecticut.

He fought in the French and Indian War. Settled in Bennington in the New Hampshire Grants (now Vermont) about 1769.

This territory was fought over by New Hampshire and New York due to overlapping British grants. Allen became the leader of the Green Mountain Boys, a militia group formed to fight against New York. He was declared an outlaw by New York with a bounty offered for his capture.

1775. Captured Fort Ticonderoga.

- Captured in the attack on Montreal, sent to Britain as a prisoner and treated badly.

1778. Returned in a prisoner exchange.

- Commissioned a Colonel in the Continental Army.

- Became Major General of the Grants (Vermont) militia.

1784. Wrote "Reason the Only Oracle of Man" (known locally as Ethan's Bible) expressing his Deist belief. It was condemned by the New England clergymen.

He died on 2-12-1787 in Burlington, Vermont at age 49.

Arnold, Benedict. Born 1-14-1741 in Norwich, Connecticut.

A troublesome youth, he ran away from an apprenticeship to a druggist (which he eventually completed) to fight in the French and Indian War from which he twice deserted.

1762. Moved to New Haven, Connecticut as a druggist, bookseller, and, later, a merchant. He was probably involved in smuggling.

1775. As militia Captain, marched his troops to Cambridge.

- Took part in the capture of Fort Ticonderoga.

- Captured Fort St John at the north end of Lake Champlain.

- Led an incredible march upon Quebec, was wounded, but continued to lead the Americans until driven out.

1776. Promoted to Brigadier General.
- Forced to retreat from Canada.
- Built a fleet on Lake Champlain and delayed the British advance until winter ended the campaign.

1777. Passed over for promotion to Major General; he was soon promoted due to Washington's intervention but not given retroactive seniority. The affair soured him with Congress. He resigned but returned when Washington asked him to join the Northern army.
- Led the relief column to Fort Stanwix.
- Performed brilliantly at Saratoga and was again severely wounded.

1778. Was made military commander of Philadelphia.

1779. Offered to desert to the British.

1780. Requested command of West Point with the intention of surrendering it for £20,000; provided plans to the fort.
- Fled to the British and was commissioned a Brigadier General; raided American cities.

1781. Denied a command, he took his family to England; began unsuccessful commercial ventures. His seven sons all held commissions in the British army.

He died on 6-14-1801 in London at age 60.

Dearborn, Henry. Born 2-23-1751 in Hampton, New Hampshire.

A physician, he organized a militia company and fought at Bunker Hill. He marched to Quebec with Arnold and fought in key battles at Saratoga and Yorktown.

1793-97. Elected to Congress as the Representative from the Maine province of Massachusetts.

1801-09. Secretary of War.

1812. Senior Major General in command of the Northeastern front in the War of 1812; recalled after losses.

1822-24. Minister to Portugal.

He died on 6-6-1829 in Roxbury, Massachusetts at age 78.

Franklin, Benjamin. Born 1-17-1706 in Boston, Massachusetts.

At an early age he rejected Calvinist Puritanism for Deism and the philosophy of the Age of Enlightenment.

1718. Learned printing as an apprentice (age 12) to his brother.

1723. Went to Philadelphia to escape his difficult brother.

1724. Went to London as a master printer.

1726. Returned to Philadelphia; started printing and bookselling businesses and was appointed postmaster.

1727. Formed businessmen's civic club, the Junta, which created, over the following three decades, a library, a fire company, the American Philosophical Society, the University of Pennsylvania, an insurance company, a City hospital, and a militia company (despite Quaker opposition). It also supported street lighting and a night watch.

1730. Married Deborah Read.

1748. Left his business having amassed enough money to live for 20 years.

1750. Began a lifelong association with science; conducted his famous lightning experiment. Among his varied interests and inventions were the Franklin stove, lightning rods, heat absorption, the Gulf Stream, ship design, storm tracking, bifocals, and the armonica (musical glass played like a xylophone).

1756. Elected to the English Royal Society (scientific) and elected to the French Academy of Sciences in 1772.

1751. Elected to the Pennsylvania Assembly opposing Penn family rule. The Assembly overcame Quaker opposition to the formation of militia companies and the building of forts to protect the western settlers from the French and natives.

1757-74. In London (except for two years) as an agent of the Assembly where he enjoyed society and scientific fame and received honorary degrees. He later also represented the Georgia, New Jersey and Massachusetts Colonies.

1775. Returned to America after falling out of favor in London. The experience convinced him that English politics were hopelessly corrupt.

1775-76. Participated in the Second Continental Congress, the Pennsylvania Committee of Safety, the writing of the Articles of Confederation, the Pennsylvania Constitution, and the Declaration of Independence.

- Journeyed to Canada in an unsuccessful attempt to recruit support for the rebellion.

1776-85. Minister to France. As the principal American representative in Europe, his role included diplomat, purchasing agent, recruiter, loan negotiator, and intelligence chief. It has been said that he performed with serene efficiency.

His Masonic membership was a valuable asset in establishing relationships in France.

He negotiated (with John Adams and John Jay) the peace treaty with Britain that included:
- Complete recognition of American independence.
- Access to the Grand Banks fishing grounds.
- The evacuation of all British forces.
- A western boundary on the Mississippi river.

1785. Returned to America and the adulation of the people.

- Served one term as President of Pennsylvania.
- Lobbied unsuccessfully for the abolition of slavery.

- Advised on foreign policy. His ever practical philosophy was that "the expenses required to prevent a war are much lighter than those that will... be necessary to maintain it."

1787. Attended the Constitutional Convention and helped to create a positive environment. He then used his considerable influence to encourage the ratification of the Constitution by the States.

He died on 4-17-1790 at age 84. His last years were painful but he rejoiced at witnessing the growth of the country that he had helped to create.

Gansevoort, Peter. Born 7-7-1749 in Albany, New York to a Dutch burgher family.[25]

Married Catherine Van Schaick.

He began his military activities as a militia Lieutenant. General Schuyler recommended him for Major in the Continental Army. He accompanied Montgomery to Quebec, becoming very ill on the way.

1776. Promoted to Lt Colonel commanding Fort George.

1777. Recruited the 3rd New York Regiment and led it.

- Sent to garrison Fort Stanwix, rebuilt it, and repelled British.

- Promoted to Colonel.

1779. Participated in punitive raids against the Iroquois; again lapsed into poor health.

1780. Sent to West Point.

- Assumed command of Fort Saratoga.

1781. Promoted to Brigadier General of New York militia regiments.

After the Revolution he was a successful mill owner and farmer.

- Sheriff of Albany County.

- Commissioner of Indian Affairs.

1793. Promoted to Major General of militia.

He died on 7-2-1812 at age 63 after another prolonged illness.

Gates, Horatio. Born 1727 in Maldon, Essex, England.

He joined the British Army as a young man and rose to Major by age 27.

1749. Sent to Nova Scotia.

1755. Wounded at Fort Duquesne during the French and Indian War.

1761. Participated in the capture of Martinique.

1765. Retired from the British Army as Major.

1772. Moved his family to Virginia (now West Virginia) at the suggestion of George Washington; became a Colonel in the Virginia militia.

1775. Was commissioned Brigadier General in the American Army.

1776. Promoted to Major General.

1777. Victorious commander at Saratoga.

- President of the Board of War. Conspired to replace his friend Washington as army commander.

1778. Appointed commander of Boston.

1780. Commander of Southern Army. Lost and retired from military.

1786. A widower, he married Mary Vallance who was wealthy.

1790. Sold his plantation in Virginia, freed his slaves, and moved to a farm on Manhattan Island, New York.

Served one term in the New York legislature.

He died on 4-10-1806 in New York at age 79.

Glover, John. Born 11-5-1732 in Salem, Massachusetts.

He moved to Marblehead, Massachusetts as a child and became a successful fishing boat owner.

1775. Appointed Colonel of an amphibious regiment of fishermen; equipped a small ship to capture British supply ships.

1776. Saved the army by evacuating it from Brooklyn.
- Ferried troops across the Delaware River for the attack on Trenton.

1777. A Brigadier General, he marched the Saratoga prisoners to Cambridge, Massachusetts.

1782. Retired from the army and returned to the sea.

He participated in the Massachusetts Constitutional Convention and was a judge and a member of the Massachusetts legislature.

He died on 1-30-1797 in Marblehead, Massachusetts at age 64.

Grasse, Francois Joseph Paul, Count de. Born 9-13-1722 in Chateau du Bar, Grasse, France.

1738. Entered navy at age 16.

1781. Appointed commander of the Atlantic fleet and supported the capture of the British army at Yorktown, Virginia.

1782. Captured by the British during a sea battle in the West Indies. After release, his charges of incompetence against his captains caused him to be banished from Court.

He died on 1-14-1788 in Paris at age 65.

Greene, Nathaniel. Born 8-7-1742 in Warwick, Rhode Island.

He was tutored by Ezra Stiles, a future president of Yale University.

1770. Managed the family forge in Coventry, Rhode Island.

1770-75. Served sporadically in the Rhode Island Assembly.

1773. Expelled from Quaker Meeting for his military views.

1774. Married Catherine Littlefield who later joined Nathaniel whenever possible during winter encampment and became a close friend of the Washingtons. They had five children.

- Organized a militia company but joined it as a private because of a lame knee.

1775. Appointed Brigadier by Rhode Island; brought his troops to Boston.

- Sent by Washington to arrange the defense of New York City.

- Serious illness kept him out of the battle of Long Island.

- Promoted to Major General on Washington's staff.

1778. Accepted the difficult assignment of Quartermaster General.

1780. President at the trial of Major John Andre.

- Assumed command of the remnants of the Southern Army and ended British influence in the Carolinas.

After the Revolution, saddled with war related debts, he was given a former Loyalist estate in Georgia by grateful citizens.

He died suddenly on 6-19-1786 in Savannah, Georgia at age 43.

Hale, Nathan. Born 6-6-1755 in Coventry, Connecticut.

1773. Graduated from Yale University at age 18 and taught school.

1775. Went to Boston as a Lieutenant in the Connecticut militia.

1776. Promoted to Captain in the Continental Army; joined Knowlton's Rangers.

After the defeat at Long Island, he volunteered to spy on the British in New York, disguised as a school teacher. He was betrayed by his Loyalist cousin and captured.[26] He didn't deny his actions. General Howe reputably offered him a British commission and, when refused, ordered him hanged as a spy the next morning. He was refused religious counseling and his last letters to his family were destroyed by the British.

He died on 9-22-1776 in New York City at age 21.

Herkimer, Nicolas. Born 1728 near Herkimer, New York.

He was a militia officer in the French and Indian War and chairman of the local Committee of Safety.

1777. Mobilized the Tryon County militia to relieve the siege of Fort Stanwix. His party was ambushed by natives and Loyalists, but rallied and fought to a bloody draw.

He died on 8-6-1777 at age 49 near the Oriskany, New York battlefield as the result of a leg wound that may have been poorly treated.

Knox, Henry. Born 7-25-1750 in Boston, Massachusetts.

1762. Employed by a Boston bookseller at age 12.

1768. Joined a militia company.

1771. Opened his own book shop. British officers gathered there as well as Lucy Flucker, the daughter of the King's secretary in Massachusetts, who became his wife and a ray of sunshine as she joined the rebels during the harsh winter encampments.

1775. Commissioned Colonel of Artillery in the Continental Army.

1776. Brought 55 cannons from Fort Ticonderoga to Boston

- Supervised the attack on Trenton, New Jersey.
- Promoted to Brigadier General.

1782. Commander at West Point as Major General.

1783. Founded the Society of the Cincinnati, an officers' society.

1785. Appointed Secretary of War.

1794. Retired to his estate in Maine.

He died suddenly on 10-25-1806 in Thomaston, Maine at age 56.

Kosciuszko, Tadeusz (Thaddeus) Andrzej Bonawentura. Born 2-4-1746 to a noble family in Mereczowszczyno, Poland.

He studied for the military, especially fortifications, in Poland, Germany, France, and Italy.

1776. He fled a love affair in France for the American Revolution.

1777. Constructed the cannon batteries at Saratoga, New York.

1778-80. Supervised fortifications at West Point, New York.

1780+ Assisted Greene in the South.

1784. Returned to Poland.

1792. Led Polish troops against invading Russians and went into exile after defeat.

1793. Became leader of underground resistance.

1794. Defeated the Russians at Raclawice and freed the serfs.

- wounded, captured, and imprisoned until 1796.

1797. Visited the United States and granted land in Ohio.

1798-1814. Tried to create a democratic state in Poland but was rebuffed by all sides.

1814. Retired to Solothurn, Switzerland.

He died on 10-15-1817 at age 73 when his horse fell off a cliff in Switzerland.

Lafayette, Marquis de. Born Marie-Joseph-Yves-Roch Gilbert du Motier on 9-6-1757 in Chateau Chavaniac, France.

His father was killed in battle when he was two; his mother died when he was 13, leaving him a fortune.

He was educated at the College du Plessis in Paris.

1771. Joined the military at age 14.

1774. Married a noble woman at age 16.

1777. Bought his own ship and, despite the King's displeasure, sailed to America to fight as a volunteer saying "The welfare of America is intimately connected with the happiness of all mankind."

- Wounded at Brandywine, Pennsylvania.
- Promoted to Major General and given his own command.

1778. Fought at Barren Hill, Pennsylvania, Monmouth, New Jersey, and Newport, Rhode Island.

1779. Returned to France as an advocate for the American cause.

1780. Returned to America bringing news of Rochambeau's troops.

1781. Sent to Virginia to oppose and pin down Cornwallis leading to the surrender of the British army at Yorktown.

1782. Helped Franklin with the peace negotiations in Paris saying "America is assured her independence; mankind's cause is won and liberty is no longer homeless on earth."

1783-89. Major General in the French Army. He was also active in social issues including toleration for Protestants, abolition of slavery, and a Declaration of the Rights of Man.

1789. Made commander of the Paris National Guard after the French Revolution. He took a moderate line and maintained order for two years and protected the King and Queen from the Paris mob.

1791. Retired when the new constitution was approved (following Washington's example) and anti-royalist forces eroded his influence.

- Returned as an officer in the war against Austria.

1792. Opposed the rule of the mobs and was ordered arrested (to a certain death). He escaped from France but was captured by Austria and imprisoned for five years. During this time his son was sent to live in America with the Washingtons.

1797. Freed by Napoleon's troops and returned to France.

1800. Refused appointments and honors from Napoleon because "popular liberties" were not being protected in France.

1814. Elected to the Chamber of Deputies.

1824-25. Toured the United States with much honor at the invitation of President Monroe.

1830. Again the National Guard commander during a time of revolution, he refused the Presidency of the French Republic.

He died on 5-20-1834 in Paris at age 76 while continuing to champion the cause of liberty.

Learned, Ebenezer. Born 4-18-1728 in Oxford, Massachusetts.

He was a Captain in the French and Indian War.

1774. Member of the Provincial College at Concord, Massachusetts.

1775. Led the Oxford militia to the siege of Boston.

1776. Promoted to Colonel in the Continental Army.

1777. Promoted to Brigadier General.

- Rescued men and supplies during the retreat from Fort Ticonderoga.

- Led successfully at Saratoga.

1778. Became ill and resigned from service.

1789. Member of Massachusetts Constitutional Convention.

He later served as State legislator, selectman, assessor, justice of the peace, town meeting moderator, and church elder.

He died on 4-1-1801 in Oxford, Massachusetts at age 72.

Lincoln, Benjamin. Born 1-24-1733 in Hingham, Massachusetts. He was a farmer.

1772. Member of the Massachusetts Legislature.

1773. Member of the Provincial Congress.

1775. Adjutant of a militia regiment.

1776. Promoted to Major General in the Continental Army.

1777. Wounded at Saratoga.

1778. Appointed commander of the Southern Army.

1780. Captured with his army at Charleston, South Carolina.

1781. Rejoined the Army and accepted the British surrender at Yorktown.

- Became Secretary of War

1783. Retired and returned to farming and unsuccessful land speculation in Maine.

1787. Led troops against Shay's rebellion in Massachusetts.

1788. Elected Lieutenant Governor of Massachusetts.

1789. Became Revenue Collector for the Port of Boston.

He died on 5-9-1810 in Hingham, Massachusetts at age 77.

Marion, Francis aka The Swamp Fox. Born c1732 in St John's Parish, Berkley County, South Carolina to a Huguenot farming family.

1748. Nearly died in shipwreck in the West Indies. Returned to farming.

1761. Fought in the Cherokee War as a militia Lieutenant; he was one of the few in his Company not killed.

1775. Delegate to the South Carolina Provincial Congress.

- Commissioned Captain in the 2nd South Carolina Regiment.

1776. Promoted to Major; participated in the defense of Charleston.
- Promoted to Lt Colonel and regimental commander.
1779. Participated in the unsuccessful attack on Savannah, Georgia.
1780. Fought many battles in South Carolina as guerrilla leader and Brigadier General of the South Carolina militia.
- Joined the Southern Army under Greene.
1781. Appointed commander of Fort Johnson.
- Fought at Eutaw Springs, South Carolina.
- Delegate to South Carolina State Senate.
1786. Married Mary Videau, a wealthy cousin.
He died on 2-27-1795 in Pond's Bluff, South Carolina at age 62.

McCrea, Jane. Others have spelled the name MacCrea, McRae. Born c1752 in Bedminster (now Lamington) New Jersey. Her father was the Reverend James McCrea, a Presbyterian minister from Londonderry, Ireland. She moved with other New Jersey people including her fiancé, David Jones, to farms near Sarasota, New York. She lived on the farm of her brother, John, a rebel militia Colonel. Hers, like many families, were split in their loyalties to King or Revolution.

David Jones joined the Loyalist Peter's Provincial Rangers, attached to British General Simon Fraser as a Lieutenant. Jane was killed and scalped, supposedly on the way to her wedding on 7-26-1777 at age 26.

There was much controversy over whether she was killed by the natives or by stray shots from rebels pursuing them. Regardless, the natives scalped her body setting off a wave of reaction among American settlers.

She is the inspiration for the character "Cora" in James Fenimore Cooper's story "The Last of the Mohicans".

Morgan, Daniel aka The Old Wagon Master. Born in 1736 near Junction, Hunterdon County, New Jersey. He was a cousin of Daniel Boone.

He worked as a teamster and was hired by the British during the French and Indian War. He was lashed for striking a British officer who had struck him with a sword and had half his teeth smashed by a native's musket ball. After the war he became an Indian fighter.

1763. Fought in Pontiac's Indian War.

1774. Fought in Dunmore's War.

1775. Commissioned Captain of a Virginia rifle company.

- Marched with Arnold to Quebec, led the attack, and was captured. He was imprisoned in England and harshly treated until exchanged in 1776.

1776. Promoted to Colonel of Virginia rifle company of 500 men.

1777. Played a key role in the victories at Saratoga.

1778. Resigned due to poor health and lack of promotion by Congress.

1780. Returned to help the Southern Army as Brigadier General.

1781. Defeated Tarleton's Greens at Cowpens, South Carolina.

After the War he became a large landowner in what is now West Virginia.

1794. Commanded Virginia militia during Whiskey Rebellion. His back-country popularity defused the situation.

1797-99. Elected to the House of Representatives.

He died on 7-6-1802 in Winchester, Virginia at age 66.

Murphy, Timothy. Born in March, 1751 in the Delaware Gap section of New Jersey.

His parents had emigrated from County Donegal, Ireland to New Jersey about 1750. The family then moved to the frontier land of Western Pennsylvania where he grew up and acquired his renowned marksman's skills.

1775. Joined Colonel Thompson's Pennsylvania riflemen and was at the siege of Boston, Long Island, Trenton, and Princeton.

1777. Was transferred to Colonel Morgan's Virginia Rifle Corps and fought at Saratoga (killing General Fraser) and Monmouth.

1778-80. Fought the Loyalists and natives in Western New York and Pennsylvania with a number of near death experiences. He threatened to kill the commanding officer of Middle Fort in Schoharie Valley, New York if he attempted to surrender (Murphy had already shot three British officers and noncoms carrying truce flags). The militia supported him, knowing their fate as prisoners of the natives, and the commander, Major Woolsey, resigned.[27]

1781. Fought at Jamestown under Lafayette and at Yorktown.

1782-83. Fought in Western New York.

He died in 1818 in Middleburgh, New York; about age 67.

Poor, Enoch. Born 6-31-1736 in Andover, Massachusetts.
He fought in the French and Indian War.

1755. Moved to Exeter, New Hampshire as a merchant.

- Led troops to the siege of Boston.

1777. Promoted to Brigadier General.

- Fought at Saratoga, New York.

1778. Fought at Barren Hill, Pennsylvania and Monmouth, New Jersey.

1779. Fought Loyalists and Iroquois in New York.

He died on 9-8-1780 in Hackensack, New Jersey at age 44. His death has been attributed to both typhus and dueling.

Prescott, William. Born 2-20-1726 in Groton, Massachusetts. A farmer.

He fought in King George's War and the French and Indian War.

1775. As a militia Colonel he commanded at Bunker Hill.

1776. Fought at New York.

1777. Fought at Saratoga.

1778. Retired due to age and the effects of a farm accident.

He was elected to the Massachusetts Legislature.

He died on 10-13-1795 in Pepperell, Massachusetts at age 69.

Putnam, Israel. Born 1-7-1718 in Salem Village (now Danvers) Massachusetts.

Became a farmer in Pomfret, Connecticut.

1755. Entered the French and Indian War and rose Lt Colonel in Rogers' Rangers.

1758. Captured by natives; saved from death by a French officer; later exchanged.

1760s. Married a prominent woman; was elected to the Connecticut Assembly.

1762. Survived shipwreck during the British attack on Havana.

1763-64. Fought against the Ottawa chief, Pontiac.

1775. Fought at Bunker Hill.

- Commissioned Major General in the Continental Army. Although brave and dedicated, he didn't have the experience to direct large operations so Washington assigned him to smaller responsibilities.

1779. Paralyzed by stroke and retired.

He died on 5-29-1790 in Brooklyn, Connecticut at age 72.

Rochambeau, Count de. Born 5-10-1725 as Jean Baptiste Donatien de Vimeur in Vendome, France.

His education began towards a religious career but turned to the military after the death of his older brother.

1740-48. Rose to Colonel during the war of the Austrian Succession.

1756-63. Rose to Brigadier General during the French and Indian War.

1780. Sent to America as a Lieutenant General commanding the French expeditionary force. He landed in Rhode Island and was pinned there by the British Navy.

1781. Joined forces with the Americans at White Plains, New York and then marched to Virginia to participate in the British surrender.

1783. Returned to France and was appointed military commander of Calais and Alsace.

!790. Commanded the Army of the North after the revolution.

1791. Became Marshall of France.

1792. Resigned in disapproval of the Reign of Terror, was arrested, and barely escaped the guillotine.

1804. Made Grand Officer of the Legion of Honor by Napoleon.

He died on 5-10-1807 at age 82.

St Clair, Arthur. Born 3-23-1734 in Thurso, Caithness, Scotland.

He attended Edinburgh University and studied medicine in London.

1757. Purchased an Ensign's commission and fought in the French and Indian War with Amherst at Louisburg and with Wolfe at Quebec.

1762. Resigned and settled in Pennsylvania.

1775. Appointed Colonel in the Pennsylvania militia.

1776. Fought at Three Rivers, Canada.

- Commissioned Brigadier General in the Continental Army.
- Fought at Trenton and Princeton.
1777. Promoted to Major General commanding the Northern Department.
- Retreated from an indefensible position at Fort Ticonderoga, ending his military career.
1785-89. Represented Pennsylvania in Continental Congress.
1789. Appointed Governor of the Northwest Territory by Washington.
1791. Defeated by the Miami Indians.
1802. Retired and returned to Pennsylvania.
He died on 8-31-1818 near Youngstown, Pennsylvania at age 84.

Schuyler, Philip. Born 11-20-1733 in Albany, New York.
A wealthy landowner and businessman, he rose to Major in the French and Indian War.
1761. Went to England to pursue war claims.
1763. returned and started a lumber business.
1764. Began settling State boundary disputes.
1768. Elected a representative in the New York Assembly.
1775-81. Delegate to the Continental Congress.
- Commissioned a Major General in the Continental Army.
1777. Blamed for the loss of Fort Ticonderoga and replaced by Gates; acquitted of all charges in 1778.
1779. Resigned from the army.
1780. Elected to the New York Senate.
1797. Elected to the US Senate after promoting ratification of the Constitution.
1798. Retired from public life.
He died on 11-18-1804 in Albany, New York at age 70.

Stark, John. Born 8-28-1728 in Londonderry, New Hampshire.

The family moved to Derryfield (now Manchester) New Hampshire while he was young.

Fought with Rogers' Rangers in French and Indian War; rose to Captain.

Settled as a farmer in Starktown (now Dunbarton Center) New Hampshire.

1775. Commissioned Colonel in the New Hampshire militia; fought at Bunker Hill.

1776. Commissioned Colonel in the Continental Army and fought at Trenton and Princeton. He resigned when passed over for Brigadier General.

1777. As Brigadier General of the New Hampshire volunteers, he defeated German, Loyalist, and native forces at Bennington, Vermont and served with distinction in other battles.

- Appointed to Brigadier General in the Continental Army and brevetted to Major General after the War.

He died on 5-8-1822 in Manchester, New Hampshire at age 93, the most long-lived of the military leaders of the Revolution.

Steuben, Friedrich Wilhelm Ludolph Gerhard Augustin, Baron von. Born 11-15-1730 in Magdeburg, Prussia (now Germany).

His father was a military engineer. He spent his first ten years in Russia and was educated at a Jesuit school in Breslau.

He joined the military as an officer at age 17, was a staff officer during the Seven Years' War, and was then transferred to Frederick the Great's headquarters.

1763. He left the military and acquired the title of "Baron" while employed by the Court of Hohenzollern-Hechingen.

1775-78. Seeking employment, he offered his services to the Americans via Franklin in Paris. Proving himself as a trainer (despite his inability to communicate in English), he was promoted to Major General and Inspector General. He directed camp layouts and prepared manuals that were in use for a long time.

1779-80. Liaison to Congress; a strange assignment for a man who couldn't speak English.

- Assigned to Greene's Southern Army.

1781. Commanded a Division at Yorktown, Virginia.

1783. Became an American citizen and was given land for his services.

1784. Discharged from the army with honor. He suffered financial problems due to a delay in his pension.

He died on 11-28-1794 in New York at age 64. He never married.

Warner, Seth. Born 5-17-1743 in Roxbury, Connecticut.

He moved to Burlington in the New Hampshire Grants (now Vermont) in 1763. He opposed the New York claims on the territory and was declared an outlaw by New York in 1774 with a bounty offered for his capture.

1775. Participated in the capture of Forts Ticonderoga and Crown Point.

- Participated in the invasion of Canada.
- Commissioned a Lt Colonel in the Continental Army.
- Defeated Carlton at Longueuil.

1777. Pursued in the retreat from Fort Ticonderoga; joined John Stark in the victory at Bennington.

1778. Promoted to Brigadier General but forced to resign by poor health.

He died on 12-26-1784 in Roxbury, Connecticut at age 41.

Washington, George. Born 2-22-1732 in Westmoreland County, Virginia.

His father died when he was 11. He had little formal schooling but showed a capability for mathematics leading to an early career as a surveyor.

1752. Commissioned Major in the Virginia militia.

1753. Sent with message to the French at Fort Duquesne.

1754. Promoted to Lt Colonel.

- Sent back to the Ohio Valley with 200 troops, including natives, to oppose the French. His party ambushed a French party killing 10 including the aristocratic leader. Some feel this was the trigger for the French and Indian War (which expanded into the Seven Years' War). The French then drove him and his small party from Fort Necessity.

1755. Helped to extricate the British force under Braddock, from an ambush. His exploits led to his promotion to Colonel in charge of all Virginia troops (at age 23!). Although his command saw no significant fighting, he learned the management skills necessary to recruit, train, supply, and discipline militia soldiers as well as to deal with the politicians and their agendas.

1755-58. Protected the Virginia frontier against French and Indians.

- Participated in the capture of Fort Duquesne.

1759. Married Martha Custis.

- Joined the House of Burgesses.

Between wars he proved to be a successful farmer, businessman, and land speculator. As a farmer, he rebelled at London's greedy control of his tobacco crop and switched to wheat, flour from his own mill, cloth from his looms, and fish; all sold mostly in the West Indies.

He acquired 20,000 acres of land in the Ohio territory. The British, now in control of Canada, opposed settlement in the West, wishing to preserve the land for the fur industry.

They pressured the Virginia governor to cancel land grants, including Washington's. His many experiences with the autocratic and self-serving British left him strongly inclined towards self determination for the Americans.

1774-75. Member of the Continental Congress.

His Revolutionary War exploits, contributions, and sacrifices need not be repeated here, He resigned as Commander of the Army, anxious to return to the life of a plantation owner.

1787. Problems within the new government convinced him and others that a stronger Federal government was needed, so he reentered public life as a delegate to the Constitutional Convention where he served as President.

1789. Elected the first President of the United States. He had planned to serve only one term but felt that the new government was not sufficiently established in 1792, so he agreed to reelection.

- As President, his main achievements were:
- Establishment of executive departments and a judiciary system.
- Establishment of an army and navy.
- Creation of a banking system and a solvent government.
- Keeping America out of foreign wars so that the country could develop politically and economically. He proclaimed neutrality in the 1793 war between Britain and the revolutionary government of France.
- Put an end to British sponsored mischief by the Western natives via military action culminating in the victory of General Wayne at the Battle of Fallen Timbers.
- Negotiated with Spain on behalf of the Western farmers by assuring trade through the port of New Orleans and by settling border disputes.
- Established Presidential prestige.

1798. Called back from retirement to lead an army being formed to fight France, now a republic and angry with our neutrality during their war with Britain. He convinced President John Adams that peace was attainable and ended the quarrel.

Raised an Anglican (Episcopalian), he personally believed in a Divine Providence (Deism) and assigned religion the task of promoting morality in society.

He died 12-14-1799 at Mount Vernon, Virginia at age 67 after a two day illness.

Washington, William. Born 2-28-1752 in Stafford County, Virginia.

He was a second cousin to George Washington.

1776. Commissioned as Captain in the Continental Army.

 Was seriously wounded at Long Island and, again, at Trenton but stayed

on to fight at Princeton.

1777. Promoted to cavalry Major.

1778. Promoted to Lt Colonel.

1779-81. Fought in South, often against Tarleton's cavalry.

- Fought at Cowpens and wounded Tarleton with his saber.

- Fought at Eutaw Springs, was wounded again and captured.

He met his wife while a prisoner in Charleston, South Carolina, moved there after the War, and was elected to the State legislature.

He died 3-6-1810 in Charleston, South Carolina at age 58.

III. British and German Forces.

Andre, John. Born 5-2-1750 in London.

He was a member of a prosperous Huguenot family from Geneva, Switzerland. He was interested in literature (especially poetry) and art.

He bought a commission in the British Army and was sent to America. He was captured in Canada and abused as a prisoner of war in Pennsylvania until exchanged in 1776.

He joined General Howe's staff, enjoyed the social scene in Philadelphia and met Margaret Shippen, the future wife of Benedict Arnold.

1779. In charge of intelligence under General Clinton. He received a proposal from Benedict Arnold (via his wife) offering to defect for a reward that the British deemed to be in excess of his worth.

1780. Arnold renewed negotiations, offering to betray his command at West Point, New York and negotiations began. Andre met Arnold behind American lines, concluded an agreement, and was given plans for the fortifications.

Andre took this risk because he was a dedicated and energetic young officer committed to defeating the Revolution and, perhaps, seeking revenge for his treatment as a prisoner of war. Fate caused him to have to return by foot through the American lines so he changed into civilian clothes knowing that he would be considered a spy if caught. He was captured by three militia men at Tarrytown, New York near the British lines.

As Commander, Arnold was notified of the captured and fled immediately.

Andre was hanged as a spy at Tappan, New York on 10-2-1780 at age 30. His request for death by a military firing squad was denied since it would be inconsistent with his sentence as a spy. Both sides felt badly about his death.

Burgoyne, John. Born 1722 in London.
He studied at the Westminster School.
   1740. Joined the army.
   1743. Eloped with the daughter of the Earl of Darby. They moved to France to escape debts.
   1756. Rejoined the army and fought in Europe during the Seven Years War.
   1761. Elected to Parliament.
   1772. Appointed Major General.
   1775. Sent to the Boston garrison.
   1776. Second in command to Charlton in Canada during the Champlain campaign which was stopped by winter.
   - Returned to London to promote his own plan.
   1777. Was defeated and captured at Saratoga, New York. He was severely criticized for the loss.
   1783. Turned to social and literary pursuits.
   He died 8-4-1792 in London at age 70 and is buried in Westminster Abbey.

Clinton, Henry. Born c1738.
   He was the son of an Admiral who later became Governor of New York. He was commissioned a Lieutenant in the army at age 13.
   1772. Appointed Major General.
   - Elected to Parliament.
   1775. Sent to America as second in command to Howe. Fought at Bunker Hill, Sullivan Island, Long Island, and Newport, Rhode Island.
   1778. Became British commander upon the resignation of Howe.
   1781. Resigned and tried to vindicate his conduct of the war.
   1790. Elected to the House of Commons.
   1794. Appointed Governor of Gibraltar, but died before taking office.
   He died 12-23-1795 in London about age 57.

Cornwallis, Lord Charles. Born 12-31-1738 in London.
 He was educated at Eton and Clare College, Cambridge.
 1755. Joined Grenadier Guards as Ensign and rose to Lt Colonel during Seven Years' War.
 1763. Became Earl upon his father's death; joined House of Lords.
 - His assignments included Aide de Camp to King, Chief Circuit Court Justice, and Vice Treasurer of Ireland.
 1775. He dutifully accepted assignment to America despite, as a Whig, opposing British policy towards the colonies.
 1776. Fought in battle of Long Island.
 1777. Key in Brandywine, Pennsylvania victory and capture of Philadelphia.
 - Promoted to Lt General.
 1778. Fought in battle of Monmouth, New Jersey.
 1779. Returned to his dying wife in England.
 - Returned to America to capture Charleston, South Carolina.
 - Took command of the Southern Army.
 1780. Defeated Gates at Camden, South Carolina.
 1781. Surrendered Southern Army at Yorktown, Virginia.
 1785. Envoy to Court of Frederick the Great of Prussia.
 1786-93. Governor General of India.
 - Victorious in the third Mysore War.
 - Titled Marquess and promoted to General
 1795. Appointed to cabinet.
 1798. Viceroy of Ireland; defeated rebellion.
 1802. Drew up treaty for the Peace of Amiens.
 - Returned to India as Governor General.
 He died on 10-5-1805 in Ghazipur, India at age 66.

Ferguson, Patrick. Born in 1744 in Scotland.
 1759. Appointed Coronet in Scots Greys at age 14 and served in Germany and Tobago.

1776. Was granted a patent for a breech loading rifle that could fire six shots per minute accurately.

1777. Fought at Brandywine, Pennsylvania with his rifle company.

1780. Killed at age 36 and buried at King's Mountain, South Carolina after the defeat of his Loyalist militia.

Gage, Thomas. Born in 1720 in Gloucestershire, England; the son of an Irish Viscount. He joined the army in 1745 and was in Flanders and Scotland.

1751. Promoted to Lt Colonel.

1755. Fought in French and Indian War; was with Braddock in the defeat at Fort Duquesne.

1758. Promoted to Brigadier General.

1760. Appointed military governor of Canada.

1761. Promoted to Major General.

1763. Appointed Commander of the British Army in North America.

1774. Appointed Governor-in-Chief of Massachusetts.

1775. Touched off the American Revolution by sending troops to Concord, Massachusetts.

- Criticized and recalled to England.

1782. Promoted to General.

He died on 4-2-1787 in London; about age 66.

George III (George William Frederick), King of Great Britain and Ireland. Born 6-4-1738 in Norfolk House, Westminster, London.

He was the son of Frederick, Prince of Wales and the grandson of George II. His education was directed by his mother, Princess Augusta of Saxe-Coburg-Altenburg.

1751. Became the Prince of Wales.

1760. Became King. He consistently sought to enhance royal influence but frustrated his cause by choosing mediocre ministers. He suffered periods of insanity which may have

been a symptom of porphyria, a metabolic disorder. He became blind in the early 1800s.
    1761. Married Charlotte of Mecklinburg-Strelitz. They had 9 sons and 6 daughters.
    1775-1814. Was King during the American Revolution, the French Revolution, the Napoleonic wars, and the War of 1812. His obstinate policies have been blamed for the loss of America although his policies had many supporters.
    1795. He reneged on the promise of Catholic emancipation in Ireland, a key element of the union with England, beginning 100 years of conflict.
    1810. He became continually insane and ceased to function as King.
    1811. His son was named regent.
    He died on 1-29-1820 at Windsor, England at age 81.

Germain, Lord George aka Lord George Sackville, Sackville-Germain. Born 1-26-1716 in London, England.
    He was educated at the Westminster School and Trinity College, Dublin.
    1737. Joined the army as an officer.
    1745. Fought valiantly and was wounded at Fontenoy, France.
    - Promoted to Colonel; served in Scotland and Ireland.
    1755. Promoted to Major General.
    1758. Defeated in attack on St Milo.
    1759. Disobeyed orders in attack at Minden and was court-martialed. He escaped execution by an 8-7 vote; was expelled from the army.
    1765. Restored to favor in Court.
    1770. Inherited an estate and took the name Germain.
    1775. Became Colonial Secretary with responsibility for suppressing the American Revolution. His poor direction was blamed partially for the loss at Saratoga.

1781. Dismissed after the surrender at Yorktown.

1782. Became Baronet and Viscount; retired from politics.

He died on 8-26-1785 near Withyham, Sussex, England at age 69.

Howe, Sir William. Born 1729; an illegitimate descendent of George I.

He entered the military and had a distinguished career although he was considered to be somewhat indolent and indulgent. His failures to pursue advantages against Washington, particularly at Long Island, cost Britain the opportunity to end the rebellion.

1758-80. Member of Parliament from Nottingham.

1759. Led the attack against Quebec that won Canada for Britain.

1765. Married. They had no children.

1775. Assigned to Boston, although a Whig and opposed to British policy.

- Led the British troops at Bunker Hill.

- Replaced Gage as British Commander.

1776-77. Evacuated British troops from Boston.

- Returned with a large force and won at Long Island although his conservative tactics allowed the Americans to escape total defeat.

- Fought battles at White Plains, New York, Brandywine and Germantown, Pennsylvania, and captured Philadelphia (at the cost of not supporting Burgoyne at Saratoga).

1778. Requested resignation of his command. He returned to England, was knighted, and promoted to Lt General.

1793. Promoted to General.

1799. Became Viscount upon the death of his brother, Admiral Lord Richard Howe.

He died on 7-12-1814 in Plymouth, England at age 85.

Pitcairn, John. Born 1722 in Dysart, Scotland.
   1756. Joined the Royal Marines as Captain.
   1771. Promoted to Major.
   1775. Marched to Lexington and Concord and ignited the Revolution.
   He died in Boston, Massachusetts at about 53 years of age after being mortally wounded at Bunker Hill on 6-17-1775.

Riedesel, Baron Friedrich von. Born 1738 to a noble family in Hesse-Cassel in the German States.
   1753. Sent to Marburg to study law.
   He was deceived into joining a Hessian mercenary company and sent England as an Ensign. He returned to Germany and distinguished himself in the Seven Years' War. He transferred to Brunswick military and rose to Colonel.
   1777. Led Brunswicker mercenaries to America as Major General. His wife, whose diary is historically important, and three daughters accompanied him.
   - Captured at Saratoga and sent to prisoner of war camps in Massachusetts and Virginia.
   1779. Paroled to New York, formally exchanged, and sent to Canada.

Tarleton, Bannistre. Born 8-21-1754 in Liverpool. England.
   He was educated at Oxford.
   1775. He purchased an army commission and volunteered for America.
   - Fought in campaigns in the North.
   - Became Lt Colonel of the Loyalist "British Legion (Greens)" which was renowned for its brutality towards both soldiers and civilians. He may not have ordered the brutality, but was, at least, unwilling or unable to restrain his men.
   1780. Fought brilliantly in the Carolinas.

1781. Defeated at Cowpens, South Carolina ending his effectiveness.

He was later promoted to General and made Baronet.

He died on 1-25-1833 in Leintwardine, Shropshire, England at age 78.

Appendix 3
The Saratoga Surrender Sequence - October 1777[28]

10-7 British defeated at Barber's wheat field and retreat to camp.
10-8 Around 10 PM Burgoyne retreats a short distance and stops.
10-9 Another short march to the town of Saratoga begins mid afternoon. Burgoyne is reported to have spent the evening drinking and romping with his current mistress, an officer's wife.
10-10 Another short march across the Fishkill River. The supposedly desperate army has moved eight miles in three days.
10-11 Cannon fire exchanged. Burgoyne meets with his top officers. Von Riedesel counsels dashing for Fort George while there is still an opportunity. No decision is made.
10-12 Burgoyne calls another meeting. Von Riedesel again urges retreat and the plan is accepted but delayed in order to distribute rations. Von Riedesel reports that

all is ready at 10 PM; Burgoyne decides that it is too late to start.

10-13 The army is now completely surrounded and unable to escape. A third meeting is called and an offer of capitulation agreed upon after considerable discussion as to how the English and German leaders would view their generals. Burgoyne states that he will take full responsibility, relieving von Riedesel's concerns. Burgoyne draws up an offer and notifies the Americans that he will send an important document to them in the morning.

10-14 A proposal with very lenient terms is sent in the morning. Gates responds with a much less lenient counterproposal which is rejected. The British and Germans claim that they will fight to the end.

10-15 A new, lenient proposal is received from Gates which is essentially the same as Burgoyne's causing suspicion among the British. Burgoyne stalls all day discussing details but agrees to sign the following morning. That evening a deserter reports that he has heard that Gen Clinton has fought his way up the Hudson and may have reached Albany.

10-16 Burgoyne and staff debate reneging on their commitment. Burgoyne tries to stall further by demanding to see Gate's army so that he can be assured that he truly faces an overwhelming force. Gates rejects the request and states that he will wait only one hour before resuming the attack. Burgoyne signs the surrender.

Bibliography

The accounts woven into the story were "learned" somewhere; the opinions and speculations are, I believe, my own although it is likely that they have been considered previously by others. In those instances where I remembered the source of an element of the story I have credited that source. The rest has come from books, site visits, lectures, and miscellaneous articles.

Following is a list of relevant books in my library - I have enjoyed them all in various ways:

    Abenaki Warrior - Kayworth
    Amateurs at Arms - Wunder
    America at 1750 - Hofstader
    American Colonies - Taylor
    American Nation - Garraty
    American Revolution - Fiske
    American Revolution, The - American Heritage
    Autobiography of Benjamin Franklin, The - edited by Labaree, Ketchum,
    Boatfield, Fineman
    Battlefield Atlas of the American Revolution, A - Symonds

Battle of Saratoga - Furneaux
Benjamin Franklin - edited by Fleming
Best Little Stories from the Americam Revolution - Kelly
Colonial Spirit of '76 - Whitney
Crucible of War - Anderson
Daniel Morgan - Higginbotham
Days of Siege - edited by Lowenthal
Diplomacy of the American Revolution - Bemis
Divers Accounts of the Battle of Sullivan Island - the SC Historical Society
Divided Loyalties - Ketchum
Encyclopedia of World History, An - Langer
English Colonies in America - Doyle
Eyewitness to History - Carey
Fighting Quaker: Nathaniel Greene, The - Thane
Flintlock and Tomahawk - Leach
Founding of New England, The - Adams
General John Glover - Billias
Hessians, The - Lowell
History of Massachusetts - Carpenter
Irish American Landmarks - Barnes
Iroquois in the American Revolution, The - Graymont
It Happened in the Revolutionary War - Bradley
James Edward Olgethorpe - Blackburn
John Stark Freedom Fighter - Richmond
Lexington and Concord - Tourtellet
Little Commonwealth, A - Demos
Marinus Willett - Lowenthal
Maritime History of Massachusetts, The - Morison
My Life With Benjamin Franklin - Lopez
Name of War, The - Lepore
Nantucket in the American Revolution - Stackpole
New English Canaan - Morton (edited by Dempsey)
Oxford Book of Military Anecdotes, The - Hastings
Pequot War, The - Cave

Puritan Dilemma, The - Morgan
Revolution 1776 - Preston
Saratoga - Ketchum
Sense of History, A - American Heritage
Seventy-Six - Moody
Spirit of 'Seventy-Six, The - edited by Commager and Morris
Swamp Fox - Bass
Thaddeus Kosciuszko - Pula
Thomas Jefferson - Randall

Endnotes

1 New York City surrendered without a shot when it was confronted by the British fleet.
2 From the Boston Globe, May 20, 2003
3 From The Puritan Dilemma.
4 From Divided Loyalties.
5 Colonel George Washington, commander of all Virginia militiamen, reported to a British captain.
6 Benjamin Lindsey, Captain of the Hannah.
7 From the Boston Globe, July 7, 2002
8 The motto on the State flag of Connecticut is Qui Transtulit Sustinet.
9 A lesser amount of tea was later destroyed in New York.
10 From Divided Loyalties.
11 From the Boston Globe, April 16, 2003
12 From Best Little Stories from the American Revolution.
13 From Saratoga.
14 From A Battlefield Atlas of the American Revolution.
15 From Irish-American Landmarks.
16 See Appendix 3 for details of the surrender negotiations.
17 Plans for a French invasion of England existed.
18 His first wife had died while he was at Ticonderoga.
19 From Irish American Landmarks

20 From The Iroquois in the American Revolution.
21 Extending the metaphor, the infant had a serious and nearly fatal affliction: slavery.
22 There were recent precedents. John Adams had written a constitution for Massachusetts a decade earlier.
23 The best opportunity to resolve the slavery issue occurred immediately after the Revolution when the concept of "liberty for all" was fresh and strong. But there were too many impediments - the Federal government was too poor to reimburse the slave owners for their lost property, racial prejudices opposed blacks (and natives) intermixed with whites, and the Southern states would not have ratified a Constitution that ended slavery. Deliberately ignoring the slavery issue seemed the only way to construct the new country although there were voices of conscience, notably among the Quakers and Congregationalists.
24 Much of the data for this Appendix comes from the Encyclopedia Americana and Colonial Spirit of '76.

Some of the earlier dates differ among the references; this may be due to calendar differences.

25 From www.nyhistory.net Gregory Ketcham.
26 Alternatively, Hale may have naively disclosed his mission to Robert Rogers, the legendary leader of British Rangers during the French and Indian War. From Boston Globe, September 21, 2003.
27 From Best Little Stories From the American Revolution.
28 From The Hessians.

Index

Allen, Ethan 38, 143
Andre, Maj John 97, 167
Arnold, Gen Benedict 38, 65, 71, 79, 84, 93, 122, 143

Baltimore, Lord George 13, 139
Baum, Lt Col Friedrich 73
Bennington, VT 73
Boston 24, 46
Breed's Hill 38
Breyman, Lt Col Heinrich 74
Brooklyn, NY 51
Bunker Hill 38
Burgoyne, Gen John 37, 59, 168

Camden, SC 112
Canada 14, 20, 38, 48, 56
Carroll, Charles 14
Charleston, SC 111
Charlestown, MA 38
Clinton, Gen Henry 37, 44, 77, 81, 103, 111, 120, 124, 168
Concord, MA 28, 32
Continental Congress 45, 112, 130
Cornwallis, Gen Charles 112, 116, 120, 122, 169
Cowpens, SC 116

Dearborn, Col Henry 82, 144
Declaration of Independence 47

Ferguson, Maj Patrick 113, 169
Fort Ann 68
Fort Edward 68
Fort Moultrie 111
Fort Stanwix 69
Fort Ticonderoga 37, 46, 65
Franklin, Benjamin 14, 89, 145
Fraser, Gen Simon 80, 83
French and Indian War 19

Gage, Gen Thomas 27, 170
Gansevoort, Col Peter 70, 147
Gaspee 22
Gates, Gen Horatio 78, 112, 148
George III 132, 170
Germain, George 108, 127, 171
Germans 48, 65, 73, 80, 86
Glover, Gen John 52, 55, 104, 148
Grasse, Adm Count de 121, 149
Greene, Gen Nathaniel 52, 115, 149

Hale, Capt Nathan 150
Herkimer, Col Nicolas 70, 151
Hessians see Germans
Howe, Gen William 37, 41, 52, 60, 77, 103, 172

Iroquois Nations 60, 63, 69, 128, 130, 134

Johnson, Col William 123

King's Mountain, SC 113
Knowlton, Col Thomas 40

Knox, Gen Henry 46, 151
Koscuiszko, Col Thaddeus 79, 116, 152

Lafayette, Gen Marquis de 122, 152
Learned, Gen Ebenezer 82, 154
Lexington, MA 30, 32
Lincoln, Gen Benjamin 111, 125, 155

Marion, Col Francis 113, 119, 155
Massasoit 7
McCrea, Jane 78, 156
Morgan, Col Daniel 79, 82, 116, 157
Mount Defiance, NY 65
Murphy, Timothy 83, 157

New York City 9, 51, 123, 127

Oglethorpe, Gen James 15, 140
O'Hara, Gen 125

Parker, Capt John 32
Penn, William 13, 141
Percy, Gen Hugh 36
Pitcairn, Maj John 32, 173
Plymouth, MA 10
Poor, Gen Enoch 82, 158
Prescott, Col William 40, 159
Putnam, Gen Israel 52, 78, 159

Quebec 20, 94

Riedesel, Gen Baron von 80, 173
Rochambeau, Gen Count de 121, 160
Rogers' Rangers 32, 40

St Clair, Gen Arthur 65, 160
St Leger, Gen Barry 60, 69
Saratoga, NY 77
Schuyler, Gen Philip 71, 78, 161
Seven Years' War 20
Smith, Lt Col 28, 32
Stark, Col John 40, 73, 87, 162
Steuben, Gen Baron von 103, 162

Tarleton, Col Bannistre 57, 111, 117, 173
Taxation 22

Warner, Lt Col Seth 74, 163
Washington, Gen George 21, 45, 51, 96, 112, 115, 121, 128, 132, 164
Washington, Col William 116, 166
Wayne, Gen Anthony 123
Whittemore, Sam 36

Yorktown, VA 123

Printed in the United Kingdom
by Lightning Source UK Ltd.
136354UK00001B/142/A